THE GOLF WHISPERER

A behavioral approach to learning golf

By

Dr. Gerald A. Walford

Gerald E. Walford, M.Sc.

First published by Dog Ear Publishing
4010 W. 86th Street, Ste H
Indianapolis, IN 46268
www.dogearpublishing.net

ISBN: 978-160844-147-1

This book is printed on acid-free paper.

Printed in the United States of America

A special thanks to Janelle Pryor Ph.D.

who knew enough about golf

and science to edit this book

The text in this book is written in three different fonts. Each font represents a different character in the story. The characters and fonts are as follows.

The student golfer is in Helvetica theme font at 16 font size as written here.

The golf whisperer is in Italic Times New Roman theme font at 16 font size as written here.

The three ghosts are in Times New Roman theme font at 16 font size as written here.

THE GOLF WHISPERER

"Ah sh—, that's it. I am quitting this f—-ing game. I am fed up with the embarrassment. All these years, and nothing? Maybe, life will be better if I sell my clubs? Hell,..... if I quit, what will I do? If I played better, it would be more fun. I need the fun. Well, maybe one more chance at this game. But, what can I do to get better? My lessons didn't work. My practice didn't work. Nothing worked. There must be something I can do? Maybe, I'm just bad?"

Hello... Do you hear me?

Oh #@%$##. Now I'm hearing things. Who's calling? I see no one?

Well you're right. You cannot see me – no one can. I am the golf whisperer. We have had the horse whisperer and the dog whisperer. Now we have the golf whisperer – that's me. Do you know me? Evidently not. If you knew me, your golf game, with my help, would make you a better player. You would enjoy the game more. You would have a better sense of well being with your game and life. You could use my help but you don't. You are trying it on your own, unsuccessfully I may add. Years and years of playing and practice sessions and you have not improved. You've had the occasional good round but over time your improvement has not been consistent. Has learning taken place – evidently not? For learning to take place you must be fairly consistent over time. Your few good rounds were just lucky.

I am with, and around you constantly. I watch you in elation when good and in despair when bad. I am with you on your golf roller coaster ride from shot to shot. I see a rising and a fleeting confidence with high ego and low ego. 24/7 I am with you – good and bad.

You do not know me, but you should. I am here to help you. I want you to succeed. You see, I am with you 24/7 because I AM YOUR SUBCONSIOUS and together we are going to get better. You have been playing with your conscious mind, the thinking mind, the mind that rationalizes and analyzes every move you make. The part of your mind that is not always correct.

I am going to talk to you – no – I am going to whisper to you, before, during, and after every shot you take on the golf course, practice range, and even when you practice at home on the carpet. Nobody will see me or hear me – just you. I will whisper to you to correct your faults and detrimental thoughts.

We will learn to play in the subconscious mode. Believe me, this game is not that difficult, so listen to me and we can make the game easier.

What – am I talking to myself?

Well, maybe. Just don't move your lips and no one will know. I am going to make you a better golfer.

How can you do that? My lessons and practice sessions didn't do it – so how can you?

To make a long story short, your lessons were filled with information overload. Do you remember telling your teaching pro, "Gee, there is so much to learn". "Yes there is," the pro replied. "Just keep practicing and book more lessons".

It didn't work did it? Now, if you are ready, we are going to start from the beginning, right from scratch. You must have a 'beginner's mind' as they say in Zen philosophy. Empty your mind of all preconceived notions on the golf swing. Your learning is now through the mind to the body – psychology, motor learning, physiology and physical skills – and the laws of physics.

Golf, like all sport skills, follows the laws of physics. Golf is a science and an art. You probably forgot your physics, and other science classes like biomechanics. Like I said, we start from scratch. I cannot assume you know anything. Like the old joke, if I assume you know something, and you don't, then I have made an 'ass' of 'u' and 'me'.

Right now you go home and think about making a commitment.

I'm ready. Let's start now.

No! Go home, and ponder it, think about it, analyze it, think good and bad, time involved, etc. You must make a strong commitment, a powerful commitment, an unwavering commitment, a commitment that will hold up under pressure of good and bad times, and a commitment that will not give up. Too many people give up when they are close to their goal. You must eliminate the possibility of this fear.

Ok, sounds good. When will I see, or hear from you again.

You will hear from me, when you are ready and not before. Remember Zen – "When the student is ready the teacher will come".

DAY ONE

Ok, I'm ready and committed. Where are you?

I'm here. Remember, I am always here.

Fine, let's go to the range?

Why?

To hit golf balls. I want to learn.

You already tried that approach and it hasn't worked has it?

Maybe not, but that is what everyone does.

Here we go again. Your methods have not worked, have they? Hitting balls is of no use until you know what you are doing, what you are trying to do and what your expected results are.

Maybe not, but ....

Einstein and others have said something to the effect that if you keep doing the same thing, don't expect different results. You need different results so let's do different approaches. Is my message getting across?

Yes.

Well shut up and listen, ok.

Boy, you sure can get mean.

I am not mean and I will be a lot of fun. I just get upset with smart people being stupid. I cannot fix stupid. Ask questions, use logic, use reason, and remember the open mind, the empty mind, - the beginner's mind.

Let' get started. I can't listen anymore. If you keep whispering I am going …

Don't finish that sentence. But, you are right. I am sounding like a golf instructor – talk, talk, talk.

Let's go into your living room and start practicing. Get your 7 iron. Stand in an open area so your swing will be free and will not hit anything. Pick a spot on the floor or on the wall near the base board or joint of the wall and floor. That spot is your line of flight, your target.

Line up your body to the target as if you are going to hit the ball, but there is no ball there. We do not use a ball because we do not want the ball to interfere with our thought process and learning process. We are not focusing on the ball. We are focusing on the swing. Later when the swing is learned we will focus on the target.

In lining up for the shot, we line up the club first. Place the club on the carpet so that the sole or bottom of the club head is flat on the carpet. If necessary, rotate the face of the club till it is facing the target. Now, move the shaft from perpendicular to leaning slightly forward to the target while keeping the club's face, facing the target. This is the position for impact. Freeze the club's position while you adjust your body to the position of the club. This is important. The body adjusts to the club. You and some of your friends do the opposite in trying to adjust the golf club to the body's position. Now, remember this – the direction of the shot is not determined by the body's position, nor alignment, but is determined by the swing. Have you noticed, evidently you probably haven't, that many excellent golfers have their feet not lined up to the target but in a so-called open or closed stance. This is their individual style for them to achieve their desired swing results. It's the swing! It's the swing to the target! Let that sink in.

If you swing to the target with the club-face facing the target the ball will go there, to the target. This is all you have to do. Square face and swing to the target. Now, if you scrape the grass under the ball you have achieved the good golf swing and contact. Just three factors –1. Swing to target, 2. Club-face square to target, and 3. Scrape the grass under the ball. It cannot be simpler. In the learning stages this is your main focus. Does this simplicity scare you?

In a way it does. There has to be more to than that. I read four golf magazines a month and there is so much to learn and do. I …

Stop. You are losing your focus. As for the golf magazines they can give a few fine tuning tips of the swing, but remember, the information overload principle. Two golfing buddies played a lot of golf together but player A could never quite beat player B. After much frustration, player A decided to do something, so he gave his buddy, player B a subscription to a popular golf magazine. A nice gesture. Player B enjoyed the magazines, especially all the golf tips. Soon player B was out trying all these expert tips. Information overload was setting in. Yep, soon player B was not worth a damn and player A was beating him and taking his money. Hey guy, you got the message.

Yeah, I got it. Swing to target, face square and scrape the grass to target. You know, I like that. It does make sense. I feel like I am backtracking and getting rid of all the baggage in my mind. My mind is already beginning to clear. I am beginning to feel freer in my mind and body. I have not even swung a club and my head is relaxed, free, in control with the simplicity. Come on let's get going, where wasting time.

Here we go again. You're starting to rush. Have patience. We have to move one step at a time and not one future step until the last step is perfected and indelible in the mind and body.

Ok. Line up to the target again. While positioning the club, many find it best to have the body facing the target at about a 45 degree angle. Your right hand is held low on the grip with the fingers rotating the club into position. Your right hand rotates, and adjusts, the club so that the face is square to the target and sole of the club is flat on the carpet. Now lean the club slightly forward to the target. In this position, your club is frozen. You do not move the club. Your body will now adjust to the club. Now swing your left side around to face the imaginary ball so that your body is parallel to the target line. The left hand shakes hands with the top of the shaft, while the left foot shuffles into position. The right hand slides up to meet the left hand and the right hand will also adjust so that it also is shaking hands with the grip. When you slide the right hand up, the thumb of the left hand will fit into the pocket of the right hand's palm. It does not matter whether you do the overlap, interlock, or baseball grip. We can make grip adjustments later. The right foot now adjusts with the left foot, so that both feet are square to the target and the ball is centered appropriately. Both feet are square to the target and ball position may be adjusted later in the learning process, but for now we will stick to the basics. Since the club was frozen into a slightly leaning position to the target, the hands will be slightly ahead of the ball – an imaginary ball in this instance.

Now just practice setting up to the ball.

There, I've done it three times and I've got it. Let's move on, eh?

Patience, guy. Patience. Yes you did it, but you had ***to think****, while you did it. No thinking. Now do it 20 times and let's work it into memory for an automatic, subconscious response for when playing, but more important, when playing under pressure. This is the first step in the building block, a part of the foundation. A weak foundation and the swing will crumble and fall apart. You cannot build on top of a weak foundations or what we call weak fundamentals.*

Ok, how's that 20 times done.

We're getting there, but you will be doing this drill along with the others I am about to give you for the next week. We are building to automatic response.

Now, take your stance. Swing the club back, slowly, to the 7 o'clock position. Then swing it forward past the imaginary ball position, to 5 o'clock, so that the club head scrapes the carpet under the imaginary ball's position. At the 5 o'clock position, swing the club back to the ball's position, scraping the carpet and continuing again to 7 o'clock position.

Maintain this swinging motion, back and forth, for 50 repetitions. While doing this drill, the mind is focused on just scraping the carpet to the target, with the face square to the target. The mind's focus is the key to this drill and your future swing.

Done. Not bad, eh.

Good or bad we will not really know until much later. We are now going to continue with the same drill, 50 times, but we will use an 8 o'clock position to a 4 o'clock position golf swing.

Ah, this is too easy. Shouldn't we get a little more technical or at least more depth. I'm already good at this.

If you were good at this you would not be such a terrible player. I know it can be boring as you want immediate results – the bane of golf lessons. Patience. Physically, you may be ok with this drill, but mentally it appears you are not. Evidently, when you are playing your focus is not on the "scrape the square face to the target." It is easy on the drill – but not on the course. We are trying to focus your mind for the shot. Like physical practice you must mental practice till it is automatic.

Your right. I'm sorry. I just have to keep working on my attitude and patience.

Ahhh, you are slowing understanding. Progress now has a chance. We are now going to continue with the same drill, 50 times, but we will use a 9 o'clock position to a 3 o'clock position golf swing.

Wow, you know I think maybe I am getting tired mentally as I am physically. It is not a mental tiredness from boredom, just an over-worked mental fatigue.

After a tough round you should feel some mental fatigue. This means you are mentally and physically playing. In time, with practice, the mental aspects will become stronger just as your physical aspects become stronger.

Now, do these drills for the next three days exactly as outlined. Do not add anything. Do not speed up the drills; just keep it at a comfortable speed. If possible, increase the drills to 100 repetitions. I had heard that Ben Hogan used to practice a version of the 8 to 4 o'clock swing 100 times every night. If he did it 100 times every night what makes you think you can do it less?

On Day 4 we are going to slightly refine the drills. By then you should have a feel for the swing and be ready for the refinement.

DAY FOUR

Hey guy, where are you? I'm ready to go.

I'm here. I'm here. Remember, I'm here 24/7.

Get your club and back into the living room. Warm up with the 7 to 5 o'clock swing drill, 10 times, and just move into the 8 to 4 o'clock swing drill and the 9 to 3 o'clock swings each 10 times.

Now, do one 7 to 5 o'clock swing drill, just move into one 8 to 4 o'clock swing drill and then one 9 to 3 o'clock swing and then repeat the three swings continuously for 10 times. No stopping between swings.

Well, I'm certainly warmed up. Would this be a good warm-up before I hit my first tee shot when I play?

Certainly. The warm-up is not the time to learn how to hit the ball. Learning is on the range and golf course, some times. This warm-up does what it is supposed to do – warm up the body to the feel of the game.

Now let us look at the swing in more detail and refinement.

Swing the club with your front arm, left arm, in a fairly straight manner. The front arm is the arm on the side of the body nearest the target. Naturally, the back arm is the arm farthest from the target. Your stance has set up the radius and the center for your swing. Now you must swing the club while maintaining your radius and swing center. If you shorten the radius by bending the front arm then you will miss-hit or miss the ball. Similarly, if you change the center of the swing you will again miss-hit or miss the ball. Remember; if you change either the radius or center then adjustments have to be made during the swing for correct ball contact. Many golfers are able to play proficiently despite minor movements of the radius and swing center as they make adjustments to the swing. Many let the front arm bend a little at the top of the swing but at contact the arm is straight.

I am saying this to emphasize its importance to the swing. For now, let's maintain, as much as possible, a stable radius and swing center. Are you feeling comfortable so far?

Yes, it is even kind of exciting. I feel like I am learning something. I am beginning to understand the beginner' mind.

Good. Now we are going to add some variation to your practice routines to achieve better balance, control and feel.

The drill now is to do your swing drills while standing with both legs together. Practice this until it is down pat.

This is not too difficult, but I can feel a slight imbalance at times.

When you have this drill down efficiently, lift the back leg off the floor and balance on the front leg only. Do the scrape the carpet drills.....not so easy is it?

Boy, I can now really feel my bad balance.

Yes, this drill really makes you aware of balance. Your next drills will really put you on awareness. The next set of drills will be a repeat of your balance drills but with your eyes closed. Close your eyes and do the legs together drill and the one- leg drill.

Ernest Jones, a golf professional who wrote the classic golf book, SWING THE CLUBHEAD, lost his leg in World War II. Within four months he played a round of golf balancing on his front leg. He shot a 38 on the front nine. His key was simply balance. Incidentally, he used no weight shift because he was only on one leg.

Gerry Hogan, the Australian golf teacher, says that the weight shift is just an illusion or perception. Each arm weighs about 15 pounds so when the backswing goes back, 30 pounds (each arm being 15 lbs) makes the feeling that the weight has shifted back. Interesting, eh.

I must repeat the importance of doing these drill with the mind focused on scraping the grass with a club face square to the target. The focus is not on the body positions.

Practice this for another 4 days and we will get back into more detail.

Wow. This is getting interesting. I'm excited. Do you think I can break par in a little while?

Patience, guy. Do not let your expectation get in the way of learning.

DAY EIGHT

This looks like a good time to explain the laws of the pendulum. Do you know the laws of the pendulum?

Yeah, the bottom swings back and forth. Golf instructors keep saying how the golf swing is like a pendulum.

But, did they ever explain it in detail?

Not really. They never have to. I assume it is because the action is so simple we all know it.

Ah hah, here we go again, never assume because it makes .... You remember don't you?

Yeah. I know.

I am going to explain the laws of the pendulum and the law of angular motion in the pendulum. When you understand this, you will understand the golf swing as never explained before. So, get your beginner's mind in gear.

Now, sit down and relax as you visualize my lecture. Picture a pendulum consisting of a string with a ball attached to the bottom of the pendulum.

Diagram 1

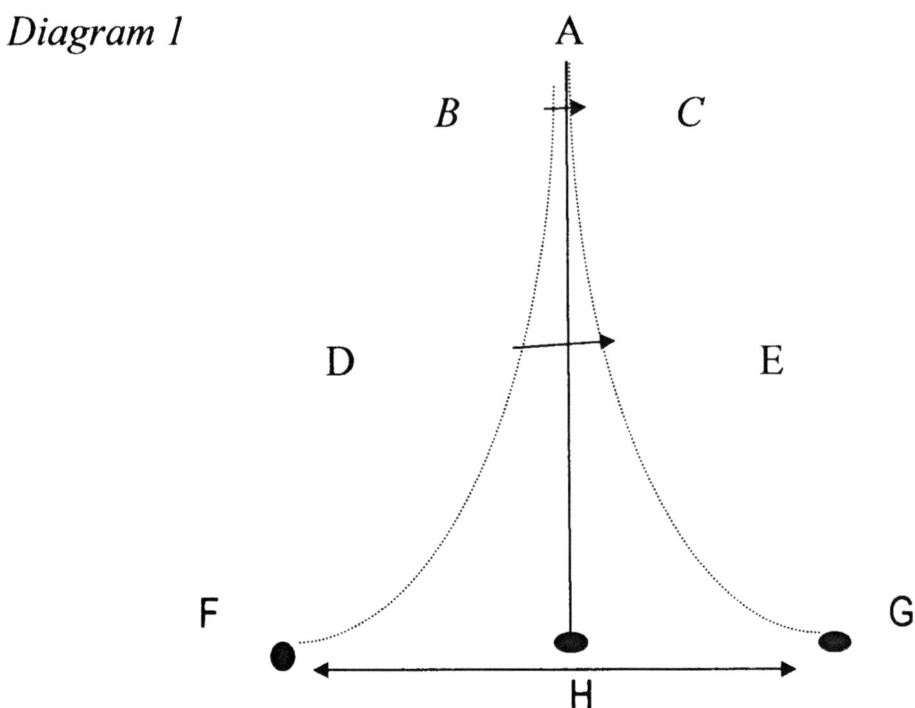

Picture the pendulum hanging with the top of the string (the swing's center) securely fastened at (A). Now picture the pendulum swinging back (F) and forth (G). As the pendulum swings back and forth, the pendulum has now transformed into an arm and golf club (A to H) as in diagram 2. In most cases, the shoulder and arm will be about the same length as the golf club, so we will say for our purpose, the hands are about half way down the pendulum.

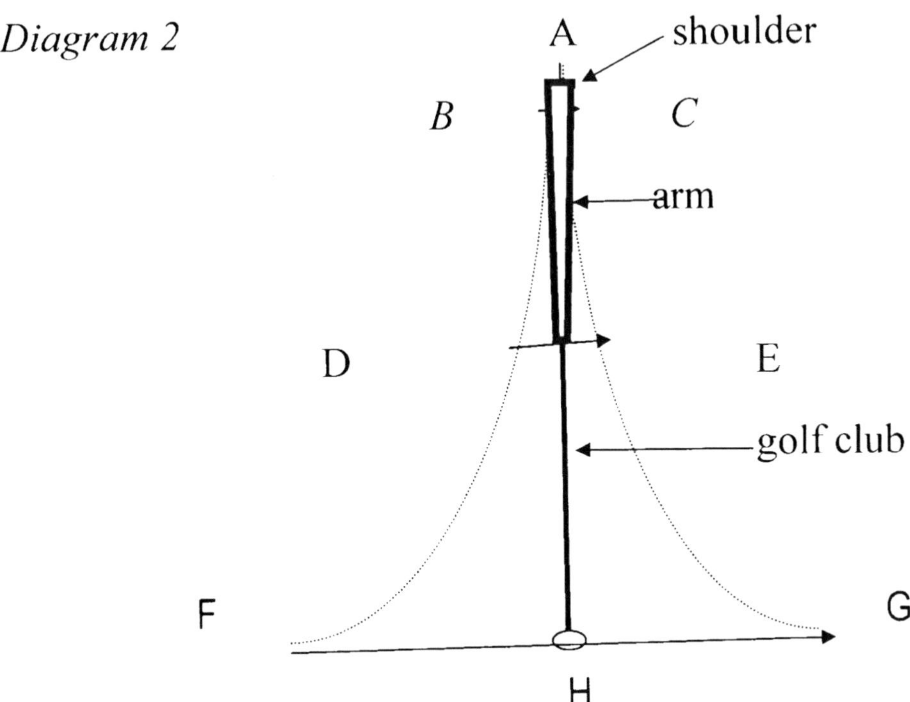

First of all, notice the similarities of diagram 1 and diagram 2.

Al the pendulum swings back and forth you will notice how the string has a curve or bend to it (dashed line). During the downswing, the string is ahead of the ball, much like the lag of the golf club during the downswing. And in the follow through the string is behind the ball like in the golf swing.

Now, this is important and the downfall of most golf swings, so listen carefully. Angular momentum's law of the pendulum means that for the pendulum to swing accurately, the speed of the pendulum moves slower up the pendulum until it is moving at zero speed, or stationary at the center position (A). The closer to the center (A), the slower the swing must be.

The pendulum has created an angle of A to F and to G. To maintain this angle of A, F and G, the pendulum will swing slower from the swing arc on up to the swing center. If not we no longer have an angle, the laws have broken down. Let's look at this in terms of the golf swing.

A is the center of the swing. B and C are the shoulders swing area. D and E are the hands swing area. F and G is the club head swing area. To maintain angular momentum in the golf swing. the shoulders (B and C) must swing slower than the hands (D and E).In turn, the hands (D and E) must swing slower than the club head (F and G). For example, for the club head to attain 100 miles per hour speed, the hands should swing about 50 mph, as it is about the half way point of the pendulum. The shoulders should swing about a quarter, or even less, than the club head speed which would be about less than 25 mph as it is less than a quarter of the pendulum's swing.

In the desire to achieve club head speed most golfer's, and you included, swing the shoulders too fast for the hands and club head. Bad shots and many slices will result. The instruction to swing slower is not entirely correct. What should be said is to swing the shoulders slower so the hands can maintain angular speed and the club head can keep up with the swing. Do this and you will achieve more distance because the body is able to transfer more energy to the club head when your timing is correct.

Now that you understand the pendulum let's look more into how the pendulum can break down for your bad shots.

A pendulum swings from a fixed point. If the center moves, the pendulum's ball will shift accordingly to the new center of the swing. The radius, which is the length of the string, should remain constant during the swing to help maintain accuracy of contact. If the length of the radius changes then the pendulum's ball has to change its swing pattern, and path to the golf ball for good contact. I am sure you have caught on by now. The center of your swing, for our purpose, is the top of the front shoulder. Various reports have determined the center from the shoulder to the middle of the neck but for simplicity of understanding we will take the top of the shoulder.

The radius is the arm and club. If the center of the swing moves from the address position there is a good chance that the golf ball will not be struck accurately unless the center reestablishes itself or the body makes adjustments. This causes more timing problems. Things like the body swaying, sagging, shifting, etc. causes these problems. If the radius changes through the elbow bending, wrists collapsing, etc. then the accuracy of the strike will be detrimental. The address position sets up the center and radius for the swing. If the center and radius change during the swing, problems occur unless changes are made during the swing. Such changes create problems in consistency of contact, especially under pressure. These changes create more variables for timing of the swing.

Is it really that simple?

Yes.

Now we are going to go into depth for a greater understanding of physics.

Now listen carefully! I have three associates, and they are all ghosts, ghosts that will further explain the golf swing in terms of Physics (Biomechanics), Neuro-Linguistic Programming, and the Psychology or Mental Factors. These ghosts are very powerful and knowledgeable. Unfortunately, few golfers are aware of them. They are always available but rarely called upon. Strange eh.

First of all let's meet the Ghost of Physics or as we informally call him, "GP".

Hi. The Golf Whisperer has asked me to help you. Naturally, I am glad to do so. If you have any questions just ask. I have broken the complex into simple terms, so let's get started.

GOLF'S SWING PROBLEMS

Center and radius changes

Problems in the golf swing occur when the center or axis of the pendulum and the radius of the pendulum change. Topping the ball, missing the ball, taking a divot before striking the ball are all caused by changing the center or the radius. If the center of the swing has shifted back, the club head path will also change. As a result, the club head may hit the ground prior to the ball, top the ball or even miss the ball. This action is usually caused by falling backward or pulling away from the shot. Similar results occur if the radius of the swing, the shoulder, arm and club change, usually by bending and not straightening for impact.

Poor contact is usually the result of changing the swing's center or radius. Such changes are usually caused by:

1. Forcing the back shoulder (right shoulder for the right-handed golfer) to rotate into the downswing too early. This is often referred to as using too much right side or right hand/arm into the swing. This action forces the left shoulder and the corresponding swing's center out of its original position.

2. The body weight not being on the front leg (left leg for right-handed golfers) for impact or the body weight falling backwards during the swing. This is often the result of the golfer's reaction to overpowering the swing. This lack of balance fails to let the weight move onto the front leg for contact with the golf ball. This error usually changes both the center and radius of the swing. Remember Newton's Third Law, for every action there is an opposite and equal reaction. Swinging forward or pushing forward may cause the body to react by falling backward as Newton's Law prescribes.

3. Bending the elbow or wrist to change the swing's radius. Often during the backswing, the golfer lets the elbow and/or wrist of the radius arm bend or collapse as it is often called. This bending action changes the radius of the swing. If the player is unable to get the arm and/or wrist straight again for contact with the ball, there is a radius change and a resulting miss-hit. This bending action is usually the result of the player trying to over-extend the backswing for the feeling of more power to the swing. Sometimes this error is referred to as wrapping the club around the neck.

Body weight placement

At contact, the body weight should be on the front leg. Some teachings stress shifting the weight back on the backswing and then forward on the downswing and follow through. This weight shift action requires excellent timing and lots of practice. Excellent results have been achieved by not shifting the body weight, but by simply putting most of the body's weight on the front leg while in the stance and keeping it there for the backswing, downswing, and follow through. This no weight shift is the new trend on the PGA Tour. It is called the "Stack and Tilt" and taught by Mike Bennett and Andy Plummer.

In support of the "Stack and Tilt", Gerry Hogan in his book THE HOGAN MANUAL OF HUMAN PERFORMANCE says that the weight shift is an illusion. Since each arm weighs about 15 pounds for a total of 30 pounds the arms when swung back gives the illusion that the body's weight is also shifting back. The 30 pounds moving back puts more weight to the back of the body to give this feeling of a weight shift.

Jerry Heard, was a rising star on the PGA Tour, until he and Lee Trevino were struck by lightning during a tournament. He teaches hitting off the right leg with the weight shifting forward after impact. This procedure helps in keeping the center of the swing stable. Although he teaches hitting off the right leg the body must not fall backward prior to impact.

Remember, the weight shift involves timing. If you must do it, then work on it later. For our learning stages now, let's not shift weight.

Wrist action

The wrist action in the golf swing is a result of the swinging action of the arms. The wrists must not be used or forced into the swing. Snapping or forcing the wrists to increase club head speed for greater power will actually result in a slowing of club head speed and an inconsistency in the flight of the ball.

Snapping the wrists counters the timing effect of the swing. For consistent timing of the swing and accurate contact with the ball, simply swing the arms and hands and let the wrists flow with the swing.

Shoulder rotation

Shoulder rotation is the key to power in the golf swing. The shoulder rotation moves the arms and helps to govern arm speed. The faster the arms swing, the farther the ball goes. The lower body rotates little in comparison to the shoulders. Jim McLean showed this in his study of the 'X' factor. The greater the difference between the shoulder rotation and the hip rotation, the greater the power to the swing. By limiting the hip rotation, the shoulder rotation will stretch the muscles of the torso for greater contraction and speed for the downswing. The greater the difference between the shoulder rotation and hip rotation, the more the muscles of the body are stretched. More the stretch, more the power.

Golf professionals practice daily and for many hours. They have good flexibility and are able to achieve excellent rotation while maintaining balance. The average golfers may have to shorten their rotation to stay in balance and within their flexibility range. If we push beyond our flexibility we will lose balance, consistency and power. It is important to stay within our limitations.

The arm roll

The arm roll is important to power and accuracy. It is not a wrist roll, as a wrist roll has a collapse of the wrists at or near contact. In the arm roll, the back of the front hand (left hand for right-handed golfers) maintains its flat or square position with the front forearm. To acquire the feel of how the arms roll, stand balanced with feet slightly apart. Bend forward at the waist and let the arms hang fully extended. Clasp the hands together with the fingers interlocking each other and let the thumbs point straight out in front. Keep the head stationary and swing the arms back and forth to shoulder height. Notice on the backswing, how the thumbs move from pointing straight out in front to pointing straight up into the air when the arms are to the side of the body. On the downswing, the thumbs return to their original position of straight out in front at the contact position to straight up into the air on the follow-through. The follow-through is just the reverse of the backswing. This drill is not only important in learning to feel the arm roll and the correct wrist action, but it also gives the feel of the complete golf swing. If the arms roll naturally, the clubface will be square to the ball at contact. Also, you will find that if you let the arms roll naturally, it is so much easier to maintain balance.

When you try extra hard to keep the ball's flight straight to the target you often steer the club in an attempt to keep the face square to the target. Unfortunately, this steering action rarely puts the face of the club in a square position. This same phenomenon occurs when a baseball pitcher starts to aim or steer the ball to the target or catcher. This steering of the ball causes the pitcher to lose control and become wild. Constantly, pitchers are told to just throw the ball and let the body flow. This same recommendation applies to the golfer's swing and flow.

The next stage of development is applying the mechanics to your body muscles for efficient skill execution.

BODY MECHANICS

If you go to a blackboard or wall and draw a large circle with your hand, you can do this fairly efficiently. Drawing this circle is easy because you simply follow an imaginary line at your fingertips. The mind pictures a circle and the fingertips follow this circle while the body flows to the movement of the fingertips.

Now, try to draw this same circle whereby you tell your body how to move the hand. Draw the circle by positioning the shoulder so that the arm has a 60-degree bend at the elbow and the wrist has a slight cocking action. The palm and elbow should be pointing downward. Now, draw the circle so that the hand is moved to the left by the elbow swinging from the pointing downward position to pointing to the right. The wrist rotates slightly and the arm gradually extends as the circle pattern moves downward. As the circle moves downward the wrist uncocks and the arm straightens. The elbow pointing slightly upwards, must now rotate inward again as the hand comes to the bottom of the circle. At the bottom of the circle the arm is fully extended, etc., etc. By now you should have the idea. Drawing a circle by this method is jerky and inaccurate. The hand does not move in a smooth pattern. Actually, you will find it difficult or impossible to draw the circle without seeing the circle in your mind. Trying to draw a circle by analyzing each body movement is analogous to the way the golf swing is taught. We teach how to move the body and hope that this will give us our circular pattern or swing arc for striking the golf ball. WE TEACH FROM

THE WRONG END. We should develop the swing path through a picture in our mind and swing the club head along this swing path by letting our muscles adjust the club to this swing line. This is how we drew the circle. There are times we must teach the body movements to achieve the swing pattern, but we must not let it become our main emphasis.

If we study the various top professional golfers, we see each golfer perform with a different swing action. Despite the different swings, each golf pro is able to achieve excellent results. Quite often, a golfer is identifiable by his characteristic swing. Although the various golfers have different swings, they all have one similar characteristic to their swing. This similar characteristic is how they all meet the ball at contact with the clubface square to the target and the clubface going through the ball straight to the target. The clubface at contact is the same with all good golfers even though their body mechanics are different. This is like drawing the circle. People drawing the circle, as earlier described, will look different in how their body moves, but, all the circles will look similar.

THE 90 DEGREE SWING ANGLE

Let's go back and take our string with the ball attached. Hold the end of the string with the elbow pointing down and the hand pointing straight up. Now, slowly swing the ball in a circle and gradually swing the ball to maximum speed. Notice how the ball rises as the speed increases. When the ball reaches maximum speed it will spin at a 90-degree angle to the center (axis). This is a natural action from the laws of physics in which an object spins fastest when it is moving at a 90-degree angle to its axis.

DIAGRAM 3

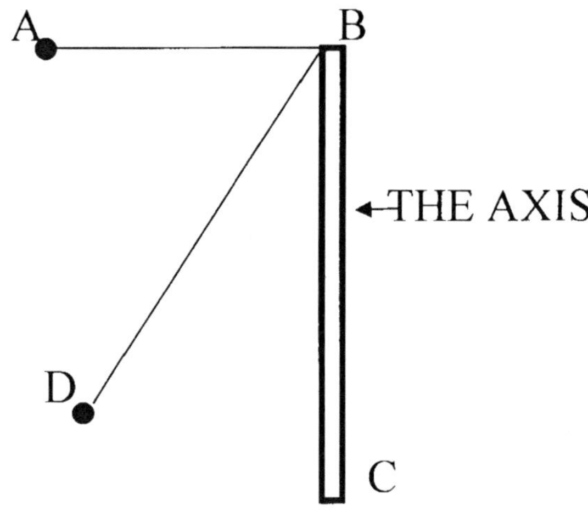

Angle DBC is not 90 degrees and so the spin is not at maximum power. As the spin increases the ball will move the string into a 90 degree angle ABC as the 90 degree spins faster.

Applying this law to the golf swing means that the golfer when swinging for maximum power should have his arms moving at 90 degrees to the axis. The spinal column is the axis to the swing. When the golfer bends over and extends his arms to the ball for the stance a 90-degree angle can be created. Some golfers may feel they are reaching more than usual but this may be a perception from past experiences of holding the hands too close to the body. About a 40-degree body lean will achieve the 90-degree angle. It is common for golfers to not achieve the 90 degree angle in the set up, but when they swing the arms will move out to achieve the 90 degree angle.

To feel this angle, take a golf club and grip it with both hands. Stand straight up so that the spine is perpendicular to the floor or ground. Extend your arms and club straight out at 90 degrees to your body and spine. Now, freeze your body and arms in this position and bend forward at the hips until the clubhead touches the ground. You are now in the basic position. You may not feel completely comfortable at first, but a few minor adjustments may help to acquire the more natural feel, but keep the adjustments minor. Feeling comfortable is not always ideal as the feeling is just different and will soon feel natural in time.

In a GOLF MAGAZINE article by Tom Stickney II and Peter Morrice their research claims that “as the handicaps go up, the setups get worse - almost always following the same pattern. For instance, amateurs tend to stand too upright at address. The higher the handicap, the taller they stand.” This means that the taller they stand, the less likely they are in achieving the 90-degree angle for the golf swing.

CHEVREUL’S PENDULUM

An excellent example of how the mind controls our muscular movement is Chevreul’s Pendulum. Chevreul’s Pendulum is also used to prove the effectiveness of mental practice for muscular action or skill execution. Make a pendulum by tying a weighted object (ring, paper clip, etc.) to a string or thread about 12 to 15 inches long. Holding the end of the string between your dominant hand’s thumb and forefinger, sit in a chair and rest the dominant arm’s elbow on a desk or table top so that the pendulum hangs straight down. Relax the body and visualize the pendulum swinging from side to side. Make no hand or finger movement just hold the string stationary. Make a vivid picture in your mind of the pendulum swinging side to side. In a few seconds, the pendulum will begin to swing as you had visualized, despite the lack of hand or finger movement. Change your focus to visualizing the front to back swing. In a short time the swing will be moving front to back. Practice changing your focus to circle patterns and various side to side angles. The better the visualization the more dramatic the pendulum action. The pendulum swings despite the lack of hand and finger movement.

What is amazing about this pendulum action is that no conscious movement of the hand is made. The hand is held stationary and yet the pendulum moves as if guided by the hand. Actually, the muscles required to move the pendulum were responding to directions from the brain, but at a subconscious level. Chevreul's Pendulum shows us that our muscles respond to our visualizations and it is important to understand that this is the basis of imagery or visualization practice. By visualizing the desired outcome, the muscles and mind respond to execute this desired outcome. The practice of imagery connects the mind and the body so that when the real situation occurs the mind and body is able to respond correctly and quickly.

The practice of imagery is like building a road from the mind to the muscles. In the beginning stages of skill learning, signals from the brain are confusing and uncertain as to where the road or path is to the desired muscles. In time, the signals learn the path or road and the road becomes a super highway. The super highway takes the signals from the brain to the muscles at a faster and more efficient path. The building of this mind-to-muscles super highway can be aided with mental practice as well as physical practice. The super highway is used by the subconscious.

VISUALIZATION

Efficient golfers are in the automatic stage of skill execution and do not swing by thinking about body movements or positions. They see the target, visualize how they want the ball to go and swing. The muscles react to the desired results. If a golfer wants a hook shot or a slice shot, he/she usually lets the muscles react to the desired shot. This is much the same as tossing a golf ball. Toss a golf ball about four yards, then toss the ball ten yards. Both tosses were executed efficiently and accurately. You looked at the target and tossed the ball with no thought as to length of backswing, arm or wrist action. Now toss the ball about four yards with a backspin action. Again, it was easy as no thought as to how much to roll the fingers or snap the wrist or length of backswing was needed. YOU LOOKED AT THE TARGET AND LET YOUR MUSCLES REACT TO THE PICTURE IN YOUR MIND OF THE BALL SPINNING AND FLYING

TO THE TARGET. This is what you must do with your golf swing. To achieve maximum golf swing results you must picture the desired outcome and trust your muscles to react as they did in the ball toss example. This trust of the muscles to execute the swing is often quite difficult, however, it is an essential requirement to good golf.

A young boy or girl learning to hit a golf ball learns through the trial and error method. He/she tries the swing and if it doesn't work, then he/she tries again by correcting the errors. The young golfer does not know about wrist break, weight shift, etc. Such aspects are skills he/she develops through the trial and error process. The child does not become paralyzed by analysis because they do very little or no analysis. The child just changes the feel of the skill until performance improves. The youngster simply hits the ball.

If the youngster wants to hit the ball to a target then he/she simply swings to the target. The child visualizes where the ball is to go and then swings to send the ball in the intended direction. The mind is concentrating or 'seeing' where the ball is to go. The mind is free of extraneous thoughts and potential muscle commands. The body moves freely. I am sure you have noticed and marveled at how free and natural a child is able to execute and learn new golf skills. As adults we must learn our skills by resorting to childhood simplicity. This chapter outlines a system of learning through feel. The drills are designed to accomplish this. You must feel the swing, and practice each drill until the feel is thoroughly ingrained in your muscles. When the swing is ingrained in the muscles your golf swing can be accomplished through muscle memory.

This stage of the swing is vital as it is the key to our full golf swing. What happens at contact will determine what happens to the ball. The golf swing is two inches in back of the ball and two inches in front of the ball. Accuracy in this four inch area will result in a well executed golf shot for all clubs and putters.

MUSCLE TENSION AND RELAXATION PRACTICE

After a few minutes of practice, tense the body and continue the short swing. Follow a few swings of tension with a few swings of relaxation. The reason for alternating tension and relaxation is to acquire the different feel of swinging under tension and swinging with relaxation. In time, you will be able to readily recognize the tension in your golf swing and be able to adjust to the relaxed swing. The skill of recognizing tension is important during game play.

This short swing drill with visualization is developing the muscles to memorize the pattern of movement. Our muscles must remember the pattern so that the muscles know what to do when called upon. Our objective is to be able to visualize the clubface scraping the grass and letting our muscles execute the golf swing. This is like putting a program in a computer and then pressing the 'enter' key to execute the program. Muscle memory is the program and the mind is the enter key.

Well it was great talking to you. If need be, keep in touch. Remember, keep it simple.

Ok, guy, how was that? We will now reinforce "GP's" lesson with non-visual practice.

NON-VISUAL PRACTICE

Practice with your eyes shut. Closing your eyes will help you develop your feel for balance and the swing. When the eyes are open, you have a tendency to let your eyesight dominate your adjustments and body movements. By closing your eyes, you must use the kinesthetic sense for movement and body awareness.

The beginning stages of closed-eyes learning may feel strange but a little practice will soon have you swinging correctly. The closed eyes will promote faster learning of the feel of the swing. Sometimes alternating a visual swing with a closed eye's swing will give you control of all your senses for efficient learning.

A guy by the name of Gerald A. Walford found that in his Doctoral Dissertation that there was a trend for the subjects who learned the 100 yard pitch shot and the20 foot putt with nonvisual learning, learned faster than the subjects using vision.

Sorry, that was a lot of talk. It could have been done later, or earlier. Whatever, you got it now and it must always be in the back of your mind. When you understand it and apply it you will realize just how simple it is.

Interesting. Most interesting. That is a lot to digest.

Yes it is. It will all sink in fairly quickly. Now, for the next few days, continue the drills without the ball. Keep the focus – "scrape, square to target". Let all this new knowledge sink in while you practice.

Practice for the automatic stage. See yourself executing the swing and then do your focus and swing. When you feel you have the automatic execution, let me know. When you can perform automatically, you are ready for real live ball action.

Wow. It's about time.

Patience! Patience! You're rushing again.

Ok, you're right. I'll take my time and make sure I am ready this time. I will have patience, pat,ie,n,ce, p,,a,,t,,ie.....

FOUR DAYS LATER

Hey guy, I'm ready.

I hear you. Get ready, we're going to the driving range to hit golf balls.

I'm excited.

Yeah, I know.

Why are you driving so fast.

I told you I am excited and anxious to see how this goes.

Calm down. You are rushing. Get calm and under control. Relax. You don't play golf or learn golf under tension. Getting to the range 10 minutes earlier will not make any difference. I bet you rush like this when you go to the golf course. You are all tensed up and excited. Rush now and you will be rushing off the first tee and later holes. Slow down now, right now. Learn to leave earlier to get to the course. Arrive earlier and be relaxed. You got that.

Yeah. I know that but I never seem to accomplish it. I will now, as I am now into a new mind frame.

Set your ball down and do your warm-up. Remember the continuous drill of swinging back and forth to the different clock positions. Focus on "scrape, square and to the target".

Ok, I'm ready.

Roll a ball into position. Use the 7 to 5 o'clock swing. Hit 30 balls.

That's 30. You want the same thing with the 8 to 4 o'clock swing.

Yeah, you're beginning to understand.

Now we do the 9 to 3 swing.

Yep.

You know, I noticed two things – the ball goes straight and with such little effort.

Funny how you say that. Other golfers say the same thing when they learn through this procedure.

Now we are going to do the drills that you did and learned in your living room. Feet together, then on one leg, then with feet together with the eyes closed and on one leg with the eyes closed.

Wow, sounds like fun.

Whew, we hit a lot of balls. Is that enough for the day?

Certainly, you did good. Over the next week you will go through the same procedure. "Scrape, and square to the target".

A WEEK LATER

Y' know, I think I am ready to play the golf course. You ok with that.

Ok, but you will have a few restrictions. You are not to take a golf swing past 9 o'clock. This will help to ingrain the swing for golf course conditions. Your only concern is to just focus on "scrape, and square to the target". Forget your score. We are not playing score. We are playing each shot. We play one shot at a time. An important aspect of golf, in fact all sports, is not to focus on the outcome, or score, but to ***focus on the process****. The outcome is the future and can only be determined by the process of how to get there. Mess up the process, falter on the process, lapse on the process or be overconfident on the process and the outcome will fade away drastically. One shot at a time. It ain't over till it's over.*

Your swing is almost ingrained. Your playing is to help ingrain your swing, so don't start to fall into some of your old habits. Just do as you practiced.

I will not be with you. You are on your own. I want you to develop a self-correcting mind. No dependency on me or anyone else. You must learn to pick out your own corrections. You must learn to control yourself and not depend on others to control you.

Yeah, ok. Wow, I just know I'm going to do well.

Not again. No expectations. Just play.

But,... a little positive thinking, eh?

Forget the positive thinking. Positive thinking only works when you have the skill to apply it. Again, just focus on your swing for each shot. Forget the' pop' psychology for now. We will get into the mental game later. Right now, "scrape and square to target – one shot at a time".

I got yuh.

AFTER THE GOLF ROUND

Ok, tell me about it.

On the first tee, I was a little nervous, or maybe excited, … maybe both. My heart beat was a little fast but not too bad. These emotions may well have been caused by all the people waiting to tee off. The first tee is tough because you do not want to be embarrassed by everyone seeing you hitting a bad shot.

This is natural. Everybody often reacts this way.

Anyway, when it was my turn to hit, I immediately started to visualize pictures in my mind of what I had to do. My drive was not maybe the best of past experiences, but it was good in distance and direction. This made me happy. I was pleased with myself. My approach and putts were also good so I made par. The first hole is easy, so I didn't get too excited.

On the next hole I did the same visualized procedure and hit an excellent tee shot. While walking to my ball I noticed that my mind was clear and unworried.

I seemed to be more confident than ever before. I was not thinking, and worrying about bad or possibly bad shots. Hitting reasonably good shots not only gives you confidence, but it also gives you energy. It seems that by focusing on the "scrape, and square to target" my mind was not able to focus on possible disastrous shots. I had the free and uncluttered mind. No distractions. The first five holes were great.

After that, I got a little over-confident. I wanted a little more distance and started to rush my thoughts and visualization. Yes, I got greedy. My mind was clouded with distance factors. I hit a few bad shots. Cost me strokes. My mind became spasmodic with fear. My energy was draining, as well as my confidence. After a few holes, I realized I was not doing the "scrape, and square to target". I reworked my mind patterns. I eased up with the excessive body movement in my disastrous attempt for more power and distance. I cleared my mind and continued.

In the later holes I noticed the same problems creeping in and I had to fight this tendency. I felt that my physical aspect seems to be ok, but I now realize how much of the game is mental. Mentally, I fatigued out.

Ahh... you are now becoming more aware of the game and its skills. The mental game is coming up soon and it must be practiced like the physical game.

I do not know what my score was. This should make you happy. I do know that when I did the correct visual focus, "scrape, and square to the target" I hit the ball solidly and consistently better.

Very good. You did some things that I don't have to tell you. You experienced self correction and were able to do it. You were learning. The mental game is just about building your swing to the automatic stage for subconscious execution. When you reach this stage, it is just simply not letting distractions interfere with you execution of the swing or putt. The subconscious can be distracted by conscious thought. Simply you must just trust your subcon-

scious. I say simply, because that is all you have to do, but to do it takes time and practice. The difficulty lies in learning till it becomes indelible in the mind and body.

ELIMINATING DISTRACTIONS

Our physical game seems to be getting under control. The time has come for some mental preparation. You remember the book, PERFORMANCE GOLF by Gerald A. Walford and Gerald E. Walford. Well, we are just going to review some of the details on NEURO-LINGUISTIC PROGRAMMING (NLP). NLP is the common name used for this type of psychology. NLP is popular in the sports world. It is easy to do, and learn, as well as being effective. Along with NLP we will be studying Zen and Sports Psychology. All three subjects are interrelated. Our emphasis is on golf but other sports and life situations are mentioned.

My second associate will give you more detail on Neuro-Linguistic programming (NLP). Meet the

Ghost of Neuro-Linguistic programming, or as we often call him, "G NLP"

Glad to be here. Let's get started immediately.

Modeling is one of the basic structures of NLP. This occurs when we model ourselves after someone. We analyze someone who is successful and then we try to imitate or model their successful characteristics. The intent is to create success instead of failure. After we analyze what is successful, we copy it. This is NLP. We learn with images and metaphors. This is how kids learn a skill. Kids look at the skill, put it in their mind, and then execute to the picture or model in the mind. Metaphors are used through examples, similarities, parables and stories that provide information and similarities to other experiences. Practice perfects the skill. Adults should learn like a kid. Kids keep it simple. Adults make it complex. To learn, study a model of the desired skill, and then simply practice it. It may be considered a form of role-playing. Be an actor. Play the part.

To learn, decide exactly what you want, and then set a clear, specific goal. The goal is what you want - not what you don't want. A clear visualized goal becomes the target for the unconscious mind. Visualize every shot to your target (goal) and let your unconscious mind determine your force, direction, trajectory, etc. Do this by looking at your target, visualizing the target while looking at the ball, and swing at the ball with all your trust in your mind and body. Your goal is to advance your mind from conscious control to unconscious or automatic control.

Once you learn the skill then you must forget it and trust it to the unconscious for execution. It becomes 'a stop learning process' and turns into 'a doing process'. 'Lock on' to your target with all your senses. Forget everything except the target. Obtain the empty mind, the Zen philosophy. Plan what is needed. Visualize the target. Recall a past successful similar shot, and with your imagination, relive that past successful experience. See it. Feel it. Then do it. Let it take over your body.

By visualizing the target and shot, you have told the body what to do. These are your instructions. Further input may be detrimental. When you toss something to a wastebasket, you do not think of body mechanics, or how hard to toss the object. Locking into the target with your eyesight does all this. The toss becomes successful. A jet fighter pilot locks onto his target (the enemy) through the computer screen on his instrument panel and then pulls the trigger. Same as the golf swing. Lock onto the target and swing. The body knows what to do. The body has been trained.

In Zen philosophy, a skill is to be performed with the empty mind. The empty mind is the ideal state of concentration as there are no mental, physical or environmental distractions. The body performs unconsciously to an automatic rhythm. The mind and body are 'IN THE ZONE'. When golfers get into slumps, or poor performance periods, they often say, "I must get out of my own way". Similarly the conscious mind must also get out of the way of the unconscious mind.

When the mind consciously controls the golf swing, the mind moves too slowly. The conscious mind has no speed. The unconscious mind is fast, really fast, and more than fast enough for skill execution.

NLP is designed to help you control your mind and your feeling. Emotions play a critical part in performance. Emotions can affect your thinking and skill execution for the good or the bad. Good emotions can help confidence. Bad emotions can destroy confidence. The mind must control the body and the emotions. Emotional control can be learned with NLP in the same way as a physical skill.

Anchors or triggers, whatever you prefer to call them, are learned when not playing golf, and when playing golf. The following basic NLP program is used when playing golf, or when a desired emotional state is needed.

ANCHORS or TRIGGERS

An anchor or trigger is something that triggers a certain response. A song may trigger the image of an old girl/boy friend. A snake or mouse may trigger fear. Sand traps and water hazards are triggers of fear to many golfers. Unfortunately these triggers/anchors are negative and undesirable. Now if a sand trap can trigger fear then why can't a sand trap trigger confidence? Is it not a matter of perception? Well it is perception and it can be positive. Pros do not fear the sand traps. The pros do not fear the sand traps because they have many successful past experiences to draw on. They have a positive perception of the situation. They know in their mind that they can play the shot. The poor players have few, if any, successful experiences in the sand. This means that when faced with the sand shot, their mind recalls their past unsuccessful experiences. It is these unsuccessful experiences that hamper skill execution as their body is being negatively tuned. This negative tuning (imagery) is sending the wrong messages to the muscles. With NLP it is possible for the poor golfer to create successful imagery in the mind to help with his confidence (emotions) and skill execution.

There are visual, auditory (sound) and kinesthetic (motor skill feel) anchors. You can develop a trigger to create a certain response. To develop a relaxation response you could slap or touch your thigh. Some just squeeze the thumb and index finger. You can do anything of your choice. But, remember you must do a different trigger for each desired response. After the trigger, go into a relaxed response. Of course, this must be practiced. Practice your trigger and then relax. Practice until the skill becomes natural and easy. Your trigger associates your mind with relaxation. Once learned, the trigger, or anchor, triggers the mind into relaxing the body. When you run into a situation where you want to relax, then just execute your anchor to trigger your body and mind into relaxing.

Actually you can use any sight, feeling or sound for an anchor/trigger. Some use a squeezing of the thumb with the pointer finger. You can create different anchors for different responses. Practice your anchor several times each day for several weeks if necessary. In time the anchor will respond unconsciously. It will be automatic.

Anchors or triggers can be developed to create confidence. The procedure is similar. You must still see, hear and feel your state of confidence. The image must be vivid and detailed. Anxiety, fear and other emotions, etc., can all be controlled in the same way.

The following is an example of a golfer in trouble.

1. The golfer's approach shot lands in a deep sand trap. He is in trouble, and as he nears the sand trap, his emotions run high and tension creeps into his body. He stands outside the trap and looks at his ball, slaps his thigh, to trigger his relaxation response. As he stands beside his ball for the shot, he squeezes his thumb to his pointer finger to recall a past successful situation.

2. If you do not have a similar experience, make one up. When recalling past successful experiences, have your eyes look up to the left, as this helps in the remembering process. If you cannot recall a successful experience then make up or construct one by looking up and to the right. When constructing the process you must also see and feel this image as if it was real life. These eye movements will usually work for about 95% of the people. If your

images are not too clear then reverse the procedure. Left-handed people usually reverse their eye movements.

3. Put yourself into the state, or frame of mind and body, you experienced when you performed a successful experience. This will involve all your senses - sights, sounds and feelings. Achieve detail.

4. Focus on the above - no distractions, no doubts and no uncertainties. The mind is clear, precise and specific. Do not let worry creep into your thought process. WORRY IS NEGATIVE REHEARSAL / IMAGERY.

5. When focused. - execute. The execution can be the swing or emotional control like anxiety, fear, confidence, etc.

Many pro golfers have set up anchors through self-talk. The golfers, prior to their swing, tell themselves things like, "stay balanced", " back slow and low", etc. These statements can help the golfer to keep a single thought in the mind. The single thought is good but not as good as the no-thought process, the 'empty mind' process. Marlin M. Mackenzie, in his outstanding book, GOLF, THE MIND GAME, says:

"Strange as it seems, the epitome of concentration is paying attention to absolutely nothing. Some golf pros accidentally stumble onto this when they talk about a "no brainer". For every golfer at every level, thinking about not thinking is close to impossible."

We'll start by whittling golf thoughts down to one per shot - it isn't so hard to achieve as it might seem. The one thought - what I call a cue, or swing key, is the thing that helps trigger a rhythmic effort. The choice of the right cue is partly based, as you may have guessed, on the form of sensory information easiest for you to process - auditory, visual, or kinesthetic - while you're swinging. It is also based on what will work.

REMEMBER

- if you performed the skill once you can do it again, and again, etc. It becomes repeatable.

- telling yourself that you executed a similar shot successfully in the past so you should be able to do it again is usually not sufficient. You must recall the past successful experience and use the mind to see it, feel it and hear it vividly.

- in tournament play, or other serious play, do not let yourself do conscious thinking analysis. Become target oriented. Focus on the target. Swing to the target. Let the unconscious prevail.

- Remember - pressure is what we create or place on ourselves. If you can put pressure on yourself, you should be able to take pressure off yourself.

There are two books that give an excellent background to the NLP program. The book by Mackenzie gives many techniques for various phases of the game. Although the books relate to golf, the techniques will apply to any sport. Marlin M. Mackenzie personally verified to Gerald A. Walford, the author of this book, that the techniques in his golf book are easily applied to all sports. Mr. Mackenzie directed the Sports Performance Laboratory at Teachers College, Columbia University. He used the NLP techniques when working with athletes in various amateur and professional sports.

GOLF THE MIND GAME by Marlin M. Mackenzie with Ken Denlinger. A Dell Trade Paperback, 1990.

MASTERSTROKE USE THE POWER OF YOUR MIND TO IMPROVE YOUR GOLF WITH NLP by Harry Alder and Karl Morris. Piatkus Publishers, 1996.

MORE MENTAL GAME FACTORS

I am going to provide you with more mental game factors. Here's the Ghost of Mental Factors or "G MF".

Good Day, Mate. I am going to give you many mental factors. You will not digest them all at once or you will fall into information overload. Take a few at a time. Practice and just work with these few factors until you have them mastered automatically. When this is done, pick a few more and do the same. Just keep moving and progressing until all the mental factors have been accomplished.

Remember – one step at a time – with patience.

The following mental factors are divided into six sections:

1. preparation
2. thought processes
3. focus and concentration
4. learning
5. performing
6. beliefs

PREPARATION

"If I had six hours to chop down a tree, I'd spend the first four hours sharpening the axe. Abraham Lincoln" (THE INNER ATHLETE by Dan Millman). The message here is to prepare fully for any task. Athletes must prepare more than they presently do. Just showing up to play is not sufficient. The great ones prepare thoroughly and with detail. The lesser ones find such detail boring and suffer the poor results. The great ones even prepare for Murphy's Law, "if anything can go wrong, it will". If there is a possibility of any happening or situation occurring, the great ones will prepare for it by practicing it, even if the chance of it actually happening is small.

Some occurrences or happenings may not be that common, but they do happen, and often the results are disastrous. If it can happen, then prepare for it. Golfers often fail to practice shots from the rough, uneven lies, or sand traps and it shows when they play.

Millman gives an interesting aspect to preparation. To him it is like building a house. Plan the house and build the house to the plans. Think of the house as an athlete. His quote is, "Learning is like building a house. The skills are the visible part of the upper-house structure. Physical talent makes up the foundation of the house. Mental and emotional talent – inner qualities like strong focus and stable motivation – are the ground on which the house and foundation stand.

The foundation of a house and the ground beneath the foundation aren't very flashy. No one drives by a house and says, "Wow! Will you look at that classy foundation!" But a solid foundation based on internal preparation will give that house, and your athletic career, a long life."

This quote is so true to the fans and sometimes the media. They like and appreciate the flashy plays. The glitter is their game. The coach and athletes know the players with the solid foundations. When the going is tough these are the players to pull you and the team through. They have no flashy moves and their ability is often unnoticed but they are the ones to rely on when the pressure is on.

It is interesting to note that golf is not through great, flashy shots. Great golf is achieved by a solid play of fewer mistakes. The golf winner made fewer mistakes – not greater shots.

COMPLEXITY/SIMPLICITY

Tommy Armour, a famous golfer and outstanding teacher makes an extremely valuable statement to any coach in any sport. "You need to understand golf (any sport/skill) in its total complexity so you can teach it in its utter simplicity." (The PGA Teaching Manual. PGA or America Publishing, Palm Beach Gardens, 1990)

SACRIFICE

Sacrifice is not a loss of something; it is a preparation for something new and better. We sacrifice desserts at our meals in order to lose weight and have a better appearance. We sacrifice time in other things so we can practice our skills to perform better in competition. Many people want to win and have success but few people are willing to make the sacrifice to achieve these goals. Such people are simply lazy and lack determination. Athletes wanting to put themselves at a higher level have to make more sacrifices, more effort and more time sacrifices. Do not look at sacrifices as a negative part of life, but as a desired aspect of life. Sacrifices will make you mentally tougher. Sacrifices tell you that you are determined to meet and achieve the next level. You will be more determined with sacrifices.

PREPARING FOR VICTORY

Tsutomu Oshima wrote the following on preparation for victory. It was good in ancient times and still good now. "In order to achieve victory you must place yourself in your opponent's skin. If you do not understand yourself, you will lose one hundred percent of the time. If you understand yourself, you will win fifty percent of the time. If you understand yourself and your opponent, you will win one hundred percent of the time."

"The opportunity for victory is provided by the enemy." Sun Tzu in the Art of War. No athlete should go into battle without the complete knowledge of their opponent. It is your responsibility to find your opponent's weaknesses.

LAWS OF THE MIND

In the book MIND POWER INTO THE 21ST CENTURY, John Kehoe tells us that the powers of the mind are governed by laws that can be easily understood. He claims that there is "sufficient evidence to indicate unequivocally that the mind can and does directly affect physical reality. Events are affected by what we imagine, visualize, desire, want or fear, and why and how an image held in the mind can be made real." Good athletes and coaches have always known this.

Thoughts or images of the mind must be repeated continuously to create the power to bring itself into reality. The power of repetition is not only used in skill learning but in mental learning. The constant repetition becomes indelible in the mind. It becomes a natural and believable phenomenon. The mind sees the results, or the desired image, so much that it becomes a habit, a believable habit.

Seriously wanting, wishing or hoping for something will not make it happen. Kehoe says that to achieve the powers of the mind one must use visualization, feeling about the visualizations and then affirming these thoughts and feelings. His book is excellent in the ideas presented as well as the simplicity of his explanations.

His visualization process is to get a clear mental picture. "Visualization is using your imagination to see yourself in a situation that hasn't yet happened, picturing yourself having or doing the thing you want, and successfully achieving the results you desire. You visualize everything that would or could happen to you and live as if it really is happening to you." Just decide what you want to do, relax, and then spend a few minutes visualizing the reality of what you want. Results cannot be achieved unless the visualization is repeated constantly. This may take weeks, months, or even years. The length of time often depends on the skill. Now, how simple can you get?

With the visualizations you must put your feelings into the pictures you visualize. Your emotions come out here. Feel as if in the present tense. Instead of saying "I will be happy" say "I am happy". The present tense creates the feeling of past successes. Feel your joy of success, your heartbeat, your sweat, your excitement, your alertness, your everything. This feeling makes the situation more real to the mind and body. The feelings are always done with the visualization process so that the process is repeated continually until it is a habit.

The affirmations are simple statements that you repeat to yourself, in self-talk or out loud, at anytime or at any place. Statements like, "I am calm", "I am in control", etc., help the mind to achieve its goal. These affirmations are like anchors, or triggers, that help direct the mind to the correct response or desired outcome. Sometimes you may not believe these statements. Just keep repeating the statement, as eventually it will take effect. Keep the affirmations short and simple.

Emile Coue, the famous European medical doctor, is often considered to have started hypnosis. He developed the famous affirmation or self-talk statement of, "Every day in every way, I am getting better and better". This statement was to be repeated day in and day out until it became a belief. This statement becomes a belief system that has shown great results in business, health, physical and mental skills.

A pilot in the U.S.A. Air Force was imprisoned in North Vietnam for many years. He lost 80 pounds and some of his health. When he was released one of the first things he asked for was to go and play a round of golf. He played exceptionally well and his playing partners were inquisitive as to how he could play so well after being in prison for many years. He explained to them that every day he would visualize playing a round of golf. He would be very meticulate in his club choice, the terrain of the fairway, the wind and any other factors to play the shot. This mental practice kept his physical skill in shape but also helped him keep his sanity during the ordeal. (Mihali Csicszenthihaly in FLOW).

"If you have a target focus, your focus is on your goal. Remember, your images become the targets for the nervous system", as said by Dr. David F. Wright in MIND UNDER PAR (Behavior Change Media, Rancho Santa Margarita, CA 92688). Wright also teaches his students to target focus for the golf shot. He has his students rate the image of the shot and the quality of the shot. His extensive testing has found that there is a strong correlation between the mind'sclarity of the shot and the quality of the shot. This works for golf and any skill. Practice improves the clarity of the image, which in turn improves the quality of the skill.

William James, the Harvard psychologist, said that, "we learn to skate in the summer and play tennis in the winter." What this means is that we use visualization, dreams, daydreaming during the summer to develop the feel for ice-skating, a winter activity. During the summer we are in no hurry to learn. We are relaxed. We analyze and breakdown the skill. We have time to put it all together. The same happens for tennis during the winter. Sometimes coaching throws so much information at us that it takes time to process it all. The off season is good for this. This is how athletes come back for the next season better and stronger that the previous season.

Hey, G MF. Let me interject here.

This is why I feel that the best time for a series of lessons is in the fall or winter. This is when there is not rush to learn. There is time for the lessons to sink into the mind and the body. This is especially valuable when making a serious swing change. Very often lessons in the spring have the learning process and the "sinking into the body" process rushed. Golfers, taking spring time lessons, often rush to the course to play and see if they get better. This rush often causes old undesired habits to quickly return. Pro golfers who practice after a bad or so-so round will have a night to pull themselves together instead of trying to get it together on the practice range immediately prior to play.

PRE-EXECUTION ROUTINES

In self-regulating sports, sports that the athlete executes when ready, like golf, bowling, archery, free throws in basketball, etc., the athlete must be careful with his routine. Watch a golfer or bowler and you will notice how the good ones go through a routine peculiar to them. It works for them. The routine is important but because it is so 'routine' or automatic that it may become boring and careless in execution. Be careful of this. Rehearse the routine so that distractions do not interfere or slowly creep into the routine.

MENTAL REST

In our quest for conditioning we often forget the mental rest factor. Sometimes the best practice is no practice, especially later in the season. Conditioning is important but it is of no use if the players are not mentally alert. Practice sessions and even matches can become boring if they occur too often. The mind needs variety. Variety helps in alertness. Keep the minds alert to help prevent staleness.

STALENESS

Staleness is a big threat in the last half of the season. The athletes become bored over the daily routines. It is the same thing day after day. Same drills. Same results. Nothing new. No learning. Actually one of the most prominent reasons for staleness is that learning seems to stop. There is no more learning. During the last half of the season, try to bring in new learning. New shots. New practice sessions. Get variety to your program. Have fun.

BODY UNDERSTANDING

When a coach, or instructor, tells a player what to do, the coach often mistakenly assumes the player will do it. The coach will ask the player if they understand and the player will say they do. Everyone thinks it is understood and all is well. Unfortunately, the mistake is made again. Most coaches know this feeling. The mistake is made by assuming that the player knows what to do just because he was told to do it. The player is correct when he says he understands, because he does understand in his mind, but his body still does not know how to react automatically. The mind knows but the body does not, yet. The player must practice the new move until the neurological pathways are established so that the mind can tell the body how to function.

Learning a new move can take a long time to be established. Pro golfers, when making swing changes, often have to wait a long time, sometimes a year or more, before the move is ingrained sufficiently to hold up under pressure. Pro golf coaches will even tell their students that making changes will take time - "so be prepared".

TO KNOW THE ENEMY, KNOW YOURSELF

To understand how to cope with, or know the opposition, you must know yourself. To know yourself and your abilities requires complete honesty with yourself. Too many players overestimate their own ability and underestimate the opposition. When you know yourself you can make accurate strategy. This is the only way.

CAUTIOUS FEAR

Very often we are taught to have no fear. In some things this may be satisfactory but it can be deadly and stupid. A no-fear mentality can lead to some stupid plays. It is not the fear that is a problem; it is the lack of ability to cope with the fear. A little fear puts the situation in perspective. Skydivers have a fear of death so they check their parachutes carefully several times. They are not careless in this respect. Athletes have a fear of being injured so they take precautionary measures like taping their ankles or wearing extra padding. Ice hockey goaltenders wear facemasks. Having no fear of losing a game or match may result in a stupid play or a stupid thought process in the dying minutes. A no fear of a dangerous hazard or situation to the golfer may cause an unnecessary mistake or risk.

Calculated risks are not the same as a no-fear policy. A calculated risk is calculated to the situation and the athlete's ability. It is a well thought out strategy. It is not a stupid no fear decision. Great athletes have fear. They just control fear. That is why they are great.

Remember: fear is a shadow. Fear has no substance. Face it. Learn from it. As you learn you will cope and the fear dies.

INJURIES

Dealing with injuries is difficult. We lose playing time and fun time. While sitting out with an injury, the player should use this time to re-evaluate their play and strategy. If done correctly it can be a good learning experience. Sometimes when playing we get so wrapped up in what we are doing we fail to see from another angle. This is a time to study and learn.

TEAMWORK

The book THINKING BODY, DANCING MIND by Huang, Chungliang and Jerry Lynch has an interesting story on teamwork. We all know the value of teamwork. In the ancient story heaven and hell are exactly alike. Each has a large banquet table with good food. The sit around the table to eat and each are give chopsticks five feet long. The people in hell struggle to feed themselves, as it is impossible to handle a five-foot chopstick. The people in heaven are not selfish; they feed each other across the table. Sometimes golf is a team sport. Golfers help each other.

PERCEPTION

Joe Hyams in ZEN IN THE MARTIAL ARTS (Bantam Books,19820) gives an interesting lesson on perception and improving the self. Joe learned this lesson after being defeated by his opponent. The lesson was on a new perception for improvement and how to look at things. It is so good that it is quoted because it could not be reworded any better. The lesson came from kenpo-karate master Ed Parker.

> Parker got up from behind the desk and with a piece of chalk drew a line on the floor about five feet long.
>
> "How can you make this line shorter?" he asked.
>
> I studied this line and gave him several answers, including cutting the line in many pieces.
>
> He shook his head and drew a second line, longer than the first. "Now how does the first line look?"
>
> "Shorter," I said.
>
> Parker nodded. "It is always better to improve and strengthen your own line or knowledge than to try and cut your opponents line."

Think about this. It is a very powerful message.

BEING TOUGH

"In order to be tough with others, you first have to be even tougher with yourself and learn how to discipline your thoughts and your actions. Whether you are resisting or yielding, in pain or pleasure, in relaxation or effort, you must never lose sight of your intended target." (THICK FACE, BLACK HEART by Chin-Ning Chu).

THE BODY

Coaches and athlete must adhere to this principle from the book, THICK FACE, BLACK HEART by Chin-Ning Chu. "A simple, but important element to learn before you can thrive among others is the ability to thrive in yourself – your physical self. A tough mental state follows a well – conditioned physical body. Hindu teachings tell us that the highest Dharma of an individual is the care of his body. This even takes precedent over the spiritual quest. Without the body, nothing can be achieved in the physical world. Put simply, the foundation to successful life is being physically fit. Through exercise and a good diet, a sharp mental state will follow."

SMALL STEPS

"Anything can be achieved in small, deliberate steps. But there are times you need the courage to take a great leap; you can't cross a chasm in two small steps."(David Lloyd George in SACRED JOURNEY OF THE PEACEFUL WARRIOR by Dan Millman. HJ Kamer Inc. 1991.)

PAST EXPERIENCES

Actors use past experiences to create the emotions they desire when performing. When an actress is required to cry while shooting a scene she will often create a distressful or very sad experience to help her create the tears necessary. To show anger, happiness, and all the other range of emotions, the actors will create those experiences from the past and execute to that past experience. As they execute to the past experiences their body language, facial expressions, movement positions come automatically. They do not have to think of these movements while acting.

Athletes should do the same thing. As the situation develops, the athlete can think of past similar experiences where they were successful and execute to that successful experience. The athlete lets the mind recreate success.

THOUGHT PROCESSES

REMEMBERED FEEL

Percy Boomer in his book ON LEARNING GOLF (Alfred A. Knopf Publishers, NY 1991) talks about skill execution. He says that you must be mindful but not thoughtful. You must not think or reflect. You must feel the execution of the skill. The movements are remembered and then controlled by feel. Concentration must only protect this remembered feel by blocking out any distractions or interference of the remembered feel.

AWARENESS

Dr. Richard Coop in his GOLF ILLUSTRATED article (July 1989 p.14) says that when a good player does not play well, it is usually because his "levels of awareness are out of whack, not because of errors in his swing mechanics." This can make sense. Bill Strausbaugh, a famous golf instructor, claims that golfers, especially the less skilled ones get too much awareness on the ball and become ball bound. There focus is on the ball instead of the feel for the swing. This ball bound focus results in a series of mechanical swing thoughts and movements.

Some martial artists achieve a state of awareness suggestive of the sixth sense. The sixth sense produces calmness and detachment even in the face of danger when fear or anger would seem to be the natural response. (ZEN IN THE MARTIAL ARTS by Joe Hyams)

EARLY DAYS

Back in the early 1900's a golf teacher by the name of Seymour Dunn wrote a book called, GOLF FUNDAMENTALS: THE MODERN TECHNIQUE TO SKILL LEARNING (Arno Press 1977 reprint by GOLF DIGEST). This is what he said, "practice by mechanical theory to form the right habits so that . . . they will be automatic and correct, but in playing. . . , the player's attention must be concentrated on what is to be done and not how it is to be done." Here again we have the teachings of target focus. Focus on the target and let the skill be executed automatically.

Seymour states that the conscious mind should be focused on the effect desired so that the subconscious mind can execute the desired effect or skill. The body muscles receive their instruction from the mind. The mind receives its instructions from the eyes. This means that the eyes must get a clear focus of the target. In many cases a glance may not be sufficient to give the body complete instructions for execution. It is best to stare at the target and just glance at the ball. Stare at the target until all the clues like distance, angle, etc., are registered and accepted by the mind and body. Once registered, just glance at the ball and stroke it. Wait too long to strike the ball and the clues will gradually dissipate.

Confidence is born of proper practice. Dunn was accurate about this. Confidence comes about with proper skill execution. Confidence gives peace of mind. Peace of mind gives poise. Watch a good athlete and you will notice the poise of his/her presence. Playing with the great ones, often helps the other teammates, as their poise and confidence often carries over to the rest of the team or individual.

Nothing improves confidence better than successful performance. Good coaches/teachers do this with their players by progressing them slowly along with increasing challenges that they are successful in. Good athletes are sent to the minors to develop successful experiences to build confidence. Golfers practice very short putts and work to longer putts as they develop confidence with the short putts. Archers do the same procedure by shooting arrows from short distances to build confidence for the longer shots. Basketball players do this when shooting baskets.

THE HOT STREAK

When an athlete is on a hot streak they are playing "out of their mind," or playing "unconscious", or playing "in a trance". These comments actually describe what is happening. The player actually **is**

out of their mind, as no conscious thinking is involved. The athlete is unconscious as the unconscious mind is controlling the body. The hot streak lasts until the mind starts to think consciously. The mind starts trying too hard. The slump begins.

QUIET MIND

All great athletes have the "quiet mind" or the "still mind". Their mind is calm and collected under pressure. They are at peace with themselves while under pressure. After all, they have been under pressure in the past and were able to cope with the situation. Such experiences build confidence. They remember their successful experiences. The lesser athletes remember their past unsuccessful experiences or failures at critical times. As long as this process continues they will always be the lesser athletes.

SELF TALK JUDGMENTS

Be careful when criticizing your play. If you make a bad play and then start to criticize yourself you may be setting up negative pictures in your mind. No need to explain how negative pictures hinder performance. Also, one negative comment may lead to another negative comment and soon there are so many negative comments that the negative reinforcement injures the brain's thinking. The negative thoughts may soon become a negative belief. When this happens, we believe in our past bad results and we have unsuccessful imagery to work with. This is trouble.

"The mind is like a fertile garden. It will grow anything you wish to plant – beautiful flowers or weeds. And so it is with successful healthy thoughts or with negative ones that will, like weeds, strangle and crowd the others. Do not allow the negative thoughts to enter your mind for they are the weeds that strangle confidence". Bruce Lee (ZEN IN THE MARTIAL ARTS by Joe Hyams).

POSITIVE THINKING

In theory, positive thinking is valuable, however in real life it can be a killer. Positive thinking cannot make the body do what it is not capable of doing. If a golfer is a 200-yard driver, positive thinking will not let him hit the ball over a 250-yard water carry. The ability must be there and the athlete must know what his ability is. Like the popular Clint Eastwood saying, "a man must know his limits".

Positive thinking can also make athletes become too judgmental of their performance. Judgments lead to thinking and analyzing and over-thinking and over-analyzing. The athlete is now letting the conscious mind interfere with the subconscious. This is back to day one. Instead of positive thinking the athletes should be using trust. Trust in their ability and what their ability is capable of doing. The great ones know exactly what they can do. They do it and the fans are amazed, but the athletes know what was possible and what they were capable of doing. The athletes just do what they can do. There is no positive thinking. No ego thinking. No macho thinking. There is no wishful thinking. No hoping. No taking a chance. The great ones just know and do it.

THE DETACHED BUDDHIST

Tim Gallwey gives an excellent description of an excellent athlete in the performance zone. "One final style worth mentioning is that of the detached Buddhist. He plays with perfect serenity, aware of everything but attached to nothing; that is, even though he makes great effort, he seems unconcerned with the results of his actions. Always alert, he shows no tension even on match point."

NO THOUGHT PUTTING

Al Geiberger, in the book THE INNER GAME OF GOLF, relates an interesting aspect of the no thinking philosophy when performing a skill. The skill is golf putting but the phenomenon is the same for any skill. Geiberger tells of how when on the putting green before a tournament someone will come to him and start talking. While in conversation he notes that his putting improves. When the conversation ends he tells himself to get back to some serious putting only to find his skill drops off. This is not an incidental occurrence but happens quite often. These experiences have taught him that he performs best when he lets his subconscious mind perform. In his words, "I've come to realize that I perform best when I'm letting my subconscious hit the ball and my conscious mind is otherwise occupied. If there is a secret to skill learning this is it".

FEEL THE TARGET

When practicing target skills, like archery, bowling, golf, basketball free throws, etc. the student should practice the awareness game. Instead of trying to hit the target, the hole in golf, the pocket in bowling, etc., the student should let it go and feel the outcome. Do not worry about accuracy but focus on the feel and how close you come to the target. Close your eyes and feel your accuracy. How close did you come? Did you miss high or low, right or left and by how much? With a little practice you will soon feel your errors and be able to predict your outcome.

Drills like these are tremendous for developing feel. Once the eyes are blocked, or vision is nullified, then the body has to rely on the sense of feel. Coleman Griffin and Gerald A. Walford found that learning the golf swing and golf putt were quicker when the students were blindfolded. To make a long story short, skill learning is quicker when the learning is dominated by the sense of feel. Learning though feel bring out the body awareness aspect.

HITTING YOUR TARGET

A world champion archer describes focusing: ". . . blocking out everything in the world, except me and my target. The bow becomes an extension of me. All attention is focused on lining up my pin (sight) with the center of the target. At this point in time, that is all I see, hear, or feel. With the bow drawn and sight on target, a quick body scan can tell me if anything is 'off'. If everything feels right, I hold focus and simply let the arrow fly. It will find the target. If something feels off, I lower the bow and draw again. If an athlete can shoot his arrow to the center of the target he should be able to do it again, and again, and again. If the archer is capable of doing it again then why does he fail? He fails because of worry, distractions, over-activation, loss of focus, and lack of connection with the target". (Terry Orlick from IN THE PURSUIT OF EXCELLENCE. Leisure Press, Champaign, IL1990)

When the program is in the brain it should be executed exactly as desired. When it doesn't, we get in our own way. Our lack of execution is as Orlick just stated.

EXPECTATIONS

Expectations are beliefs in outcomes, thinking of the future. Remember you must stay in the present. Forget your expectations. Work on the present. Expectations are distraction to the present. You cannot get into the future if you do not cope with the present. Striving for an expectation creates more pressure. It creates a trying too hard syndrome. Stay in the present. Live the present.

Some may think they have to have expectations in order to make their plans. Not really. Your plans are for execution and not for outcomes. You play for the moment, the present, and let the outcome happen. When the outcome happens then you must play the present again and keep playing the present.

"As soon as you put a value on a putt, shot, round, or tournament you lose your present focus, your thoughts advance to the future, your nervous system accelerates, and concentration skills diminish as your physical movement and swing tempo quickens." Dr. David F. Wright, in MIND UNDER PAR, discusses the importance of staying in the present for any skill.

"Never collect any trophies in your head until you have them in your hand." Sam Snead in THE EDUCATION OF A GOLFER. Simon and Schuster, NY 1961.

At the Masters golf tournament in 1961 Arnold Palmer was the defending champion. As he walked up the 18th fairway with a one stroke lead he accepted premature congratulations from George Low, an outstanding putting teacher. When he was ready to play his shot he said, "I was suddenly unsure about what I should be thinking about. Instead of seeing nothing around me, except the business at hand. . . I suddenly seemed to notice everything around me, the color of the sky, the expectant faces of the people in the gallery, you name it." His shot went into the bunker. His sand shot out of the bunker was skulled (hit thin) across the green. He got a double bogey (two shots over par for the hole). He lost the tournament. "What really tore me up inside was the knowledge that I'd lost because I'd failed to do what Pap had always told me to do – stay focused until the job is finished" (from the book A GOLFER'S LIFE by Arnold Palmer).

LOWER MIND/HIGHER MIND

Grand Master Richard Behrens in his interesting, and valuable book GOLF - THE WINNER'S WAY, APPLYING THE TEACHINGS OF MARTIAL ARTS, Llewellyn Publications, St. Paul, MN 1999, talks about results in his teaching. Behrens has worked with pro athletes in NBA, NFL, PGA and the Olympics.

Behrens claims that no matter the sport the lower mind (conscious mind) is common to all sports. Control of the lower mind is the key to excellence. His teachings stress control of the lower mind so the higher mind (the subconscious mind) can take control of skill execution. This helps to confirm that control over the lower mind or the conscious mind is the key to skill execution no matter the sport or activity.

The lower mind will not "shut up". It will constantly interfere with instructions and distractions. "An undisciplined lower mind is a golfer's greatest enemy. The higher mind is infallible, accurate, peaceful and serene. "It is the higher mind that an athlete uses when he or she is in the 'zone'.

RESULTS

"In the martial arts, we never look for results. We learn, sometimes painfully, that if we execute our techniques correctly, positive results will occur automatically. You must not preoccupy yourself with final results while you are executing your techniques and employing your principles, you must learn to do what you are doing, in the moment, that you are doing them." Richard Behrens in his book GOLF, THE WINNER'S WAY, APPLYING THE TEACHINGS OF MARTIAL ARTS, Llewellyn Publications, St. Paul, Mn 1999.

Davis Love III in Golf Magazine (Feb.2001, p. 160) was asked what does trying too hard mean. He replied, "It means going out with a score in mind. It means watching the scoreboard and changing your game plan or attitude. It is letting results and goals and outside influences change the way you play."

STOP THINKING

"Stop thinking about the shot!" the master called out. "That way it is bound to fail."

"I can't help it," I answered, "the tension gets too painful."

"You only feel it because you haven't really let go of yourself. It is all so simple."

The above quotes are from the book ZEN IN THE ART OF ARCHERY. The conversation is between the master and the student. Eugen Herrigel is the student and author who is learning the skill of archery. The skill of letting go applies to all sports and skills.

Herrigel also talks about how the master refers to hitting the target as just a confirmation of the shooter's ego; the vanity of the shot is almost an act of showing off. The master is trying to get Herrigel to understand that the results of the shot must not be in the mind when the mind should be on the execution, on the moment and not on the results or outcome.

Herrigel also asks about why it is taking him so long to grasp the concept of letting go. The master's reply is, "The way to the goal is not to be measured! Of what importance are weeks, months, years?" The concept of letting go was how the master aimed or rather did not aim. Aiming was with no formal procedure of 'do this, do that'. Aiming was a letting the body do it.

Herrigel then went on to watch his master demonstrate hitting a target in the distance in the dark. In fact both arrows hit the center and the second arrow actually split the first arrow. How did the master do it without aiming? The target was in the dark. He did it without the interference from the aiming thought process.

Fred Couples, the famous golfer, when asked how he aims, replied that when he is playing well he does not really aim. He just plays to the target. Hockey, basketball, and soccer players don't really aim at the goal. They let it go. They know where the openings are. Great athletes let go. The authors were watching a basketball game on TV and Michael Jordan closed his eyes and sank the free throw. He did not aim. He let it happen. It happened naturally. The end result was good.

Two famous golfers, Chi Chi Rodriquez and Ralph Guldahl_became victims to thinking analysis. Chi Chi was asked to write an article on putting and Frank was asked to write a book on the golf swing. Both golfers became so engrossed in the mechanics that they never played the same again. They became victims of mechanics, victims of over analysis.

GUILT

"When you have guilt, fear, anxiety, regret and/or nervous anticipation, you are living in the past or the future. You must live now, in the present, in this moment." From the THE BOOK OF FIVE RINGS.

CENTERING

Being centered is a form of balance. It means being centered between two extremes. It is a balance of an extreme at each end of the spectrum. Center your emotions. Do not be overly excited and do not be overly mundane. Be in the center of these extremes. If you are overly excited your skill level may be hampered. If you are overly mundane (don't care) then your skill level will be hampered. By being centered, you will be able to remain calm, cool and collected. You will see the big picture. Your muscles will be able to respond efficiently. Your mind will be able to reason and respond to the situation correctly.

FAILURE

The arrow that hits the bull's eye is the result of a hundred misses. Success does not come easy, especially in sports. There are a lot of failures before success. The great ones did not quit. They believed that they could eventually overcome their failures. They stuck with it. Sports are like a ride on a roller coaster. There are up and downs. The good ones know and learn how to handle the downs. Most people are ok when everything is going their way. Coping with the bad times separates the strong from the weak. We learned to walk after many repeated failures. We did not quit. It is almost as if failure was our teacher. Failure makes us better. Failure is not failure; it is part of the learning process. Treat it as such.

SELF-MOTIVATION

"Studies of Olympic athletes, world class musicians, and chess grand masters find that their unifying trait is the ability to motivate themselves to pursue relentless training routines." (EMOTIONAL INTELLIGENCE by Daniel Goleman. Bantam Books, NY 1995).

Good coaches are not motivators. They merely do not stiffen the motivation of their player (s). Coaches often hamper the motivation of the athlete. An athlete is motivated - they should be. Motivation is an internal thing. You can lead a horse to water but you can't make him drink. An athlete, in fact anyone, cannot be motivated if they do not want to be motivated.

TALK IN PICTURES

Good coaches explain things in pictures. Their verbal explanation creates a picture in the mind of the student. The student then has the picture in the mind. The language of the mind has been established. Once the picture in the mind is set, the instructor can then proceed to working on the feel of the skill and not a "do this - do that" mentality. The student is now able to experience the skill and not just try the skill.

JUDGMENTS

Negative judgments create bad pictures in the mind. It clouds our vision and image. It just tries to tell us we are doing bad, or wrong, but it does not tell us what to correct. This creates doubt and uncertainty. So what good are they?

Positive judgments, although better, may create carelessness as we just shrug off our problem with a false sense of security that we have it corrected or under control. Very often we don't. Use positive judgments but keep them under control.

TIME OF THOUGHT

Taisen Deshimaru in his book THE ZEN WAY TO THE MARTIAL ARTS writes about how a samurai chooses a technique of attack in sword-fighting. His answer also applies to sport. "There is no choosing. It happens unconsciously, automatically, naturally. There can be no thought, because if there is a thought, there is a time of thought, and that means a flaw. For the right movement to occur there must be permanent, totally alert awareness, of the entire situation; that awareness chooses the right stroke, technique, and body to execute it, and it is all over. . . But if you take time to think, “I must use this or that technique,” you will be struck while you are thinking. Intuition triggers body and technique. Body and consciousness unite; you think with the whole body, your whole self is invested in the reaction.”

FOCUS AND CONCENTRATION

THE MIND’S EYE

The mind’s eye is the visualization or imagery process where the athlete pictures the target and keeps the picture in the mind while executing the skill. This may well be the trigger to entering the zone. The great ones picture the target, feel the experience and then do the skill – unconsciously. The picture of the target signals the mind as to what must be done. The mind sends signals to the muscles and then the muscles react. It is that simple, so keep it that simple. Do not get caught up in how to execute. You already know how. Just do it.

Bill Russell, the all time great basketball player, tells of how he used mental imagery to help improve his game when he was 18 years old. “Something happened that night that opened my eyes and chilled my spine. I was sitting on the bench watching Treu and McKelvey the way I always did. Every time one of them would make one of those moves I liked, I'd close my eyes just afterward and try to see the play in my mind. In other words, I'd try to create an instant replay on the inside of my eyelids. Usually, I'd catch only a part of a particular move the first time I'd try this; I'd miss the headwork or the way the ball was carried or maybe the sequence of steps. But the next time I saw the move I'd catch a little more of it, so that soon I could call up a complete picture. On this particular night I was working on replays of many plays, including McKelvey's way of taking an offensive rebound and moving quickly to the hoop. It's a fairly simple play for any big man in basketball, but I didn't execute it well and McKelvey did. Since I had an accurate vision of his technique in my head, I started playing with the image right there on the bench, running back the picture several times and each time inserting a part of me for McKelvey. Finally I saw myself making the whole move, and I ran this over and over. When I went in the game, I grabbed an offensive rebound and put it in the basket just the way McKelvey did. It seemed natural, almost as if I were just stepping into a film, and following the signs. When the imitation worked and the ball went in, I could barely contain myself. I was so elated I thought I would float right out of the gym. Now for the first time I had transferred something from my head to my body. It seemed so easy. My first dose of athletic confidence was coming to me when I was 18 years old. (SECOND WIND by Bill Russell and T. Branch. Ballantine, NY, 1979).

CATCH THE BALL

Tim Gallwey, the author of THE INNER GAME OF TENNIS and THE INNER GAME OF GOLF (Random House, NY), did an interesting experiment at one of his seminars. He asked for someone who could not catch a ball. A lady volunteered. He tossed her a ball several times to confirm that she could not catch. He then proceeded to tell her to watch the ball and don't think about trying to catch the ball. Just count how many times the ball rotates. Each time the ball was tossed the lady called out the number of rotations as she caught the ball. After a very few catches she realized that she was catching the ball and was in total disbelief that she actually was able to do the skill.

What is interesting about this experiment is that the lady could catch the ball when she did not think about how to catch the ball. Counting the revolutions of the ball changed her focus from trying, or forcing to catch the ball, to doing it subconsciously. Gallway discovered in his teaching of tennis. His students performed better at hitting the ball when they focused on the self-talk of 'back – hit" to perform the stroke rather than thinking of the many body mechanics of the skill. The "back – hit" was a means of clearing the mind of swing mechanics so the body could let go.

PERFORMANCE BREATHING

In Aikido, a martial art, breathing makes the mind clearer. Smooth deep breaths can help the body to respond smoothly and in control. One of the keys is to breathe in when getting ready to execute a powerful move, and then exhale during the execution. Jimmy Connors, and other tennis players, grunt and expel air with their contact with the ball. The martial artists do this when breaking boards, bricks, etc. Golfers may be encouraged to do this. Such action gives the body more power, but it does take practice.

Taisen Deshimaru recommends this test to experience this breathing skill. He says to lift a heavy weight while breathing in. Now lift the weight while breathing out. You will feel the difference. You are stronger breathing out.

TRYING TOO RELAX

Athletes, when practicing, often feel they found the secret, only to find that the next day or next time out playing they revert back to their old bad habits. What happens is that the player tries too hard to repeat the feel from yesterday. The more they try, the more it gets worse. They are then told to relax and let it happen. When they let it happen, they get too careless, too easy going, and off-focus. Relaxing is not really relaxing. Relax too much and you go limp and useless. To relax you must just let it happen. Force relaxation and it will never come. In fact, the body will just get tighter.

FOCUS ON THE SPOT

Baseball players, golfers, tennis players, etc. are told to watch the ball. In recent years the players are now told to focus on a dimple on the golf ball, or the seam on a baseball, softball or tennis ball. It seems that be focusing on the dimple or seam the concentration of the athlete becomes so focused on the ball that thoughts of how to hit the ball are not able to get into the mind and cause problems. This technique helps the performer to “let go” and “let it happen”.

CONCENTRATION

Practice concentration but don't just practice concentration to improve in your sport. Use your sport to improve your concentration. When you do this you will find concentration carries over into other life situations.

Relaxation and concentration go hand in hand. Too much concentration defeats itself. Allow the body and the unconscious to do their share in concentrating. Do not let the conscious mind take control, concentration can become effortless effort. Joe Hyams could not quite grasp this physically, although mentally he understood the philosophy. While he was playing tennis he noticed how when the opponent's serve was a little long out of the service area he would return it back with a good shot. After doing this several times he noticed what was meant by the relaxation and concentration skill. When the opponent's serve was out Joe did not have to try hard to return the ball. He did not tighten up, strain and over concentrate. He simply reacted by letting his skill happen. It happened. In his words, "When I stopped straining, it happened. I had made the breakthrough."

"The less effort, the faster and more powerful you will be." (Bruce Lee from ZEN IN THE MARTIAL ARTS by Joe Hyams).

"Concentration is like breathing – you never think about it. The roof could fall in and, if it missed you, you would be unaware of it." A statement by a chess player from the book FLOW by Mihali Csikszent-mihali.

"Your concentration is very complete. Your mind isn't wandering, you are not thinking of something else; you are totally involved in what you are doing. . . Your energy is flowing very smoothly. You feel relaxed, comfortable and energetic". A statement by a dancer from the book FLOW by Mihali Csik-szentmihali.

Chess players and players in other so called non physical activities train for their activity with demanding physical activity like running, swimming and bike riding. They have found that good physical conditioning helps them to concentrate longer and better. Chess is one of the most cerebral activities. With its high levels of concentration, for long periods of time, physical fitness is needed. Physical fitness helps mental fitness and stamina.

CONCENTRATION and AWARENESS

Concentration is the complete focus on the task. Awareness is the perception of what is going on around you. The two are compatible. Good athletes are able to concentrate or focus on the task, while maintaining awareness on the surroundings or environment. A football quarterback focuses on his receiver but has to be aware of the charging opposition. Putting awareness and concentration together is not easy. It takes practice and time. This is essential. A player cannot become great until these two factors can be achieved simultaneously.

Learning to concentrate takes practice. There is no trick. Just practice it. But, remember, focus on the task and do not concentrate on concentrating. No force. No effort. It is easy and natural. Just focus on the task and do let distractions interfere. Provide the opportunity to let it happen.

Terry Orlick gives an interesting example of focusing. He says to watch a young child play. There is no strain or stress. The body is relaxed and the mind is not distracted from their focus on playing. The child, pushing the little truck, is totally absorbed in the truck. The absorption is easy, natural and flowing. A 14 year old girl into competitive fiqure skating saw Orlick for help because she lost her focus.

When she was 11 years old she performed like the child playing. Totally absorbed like the child pushing the little truck. At 11 she had no problems. She just performed. When she got older she started to think of the judges, audience, other skaters, evaluations, etc. She started to think of winning because it was stressed and discussed by others. It began to play on her mind. All these distractions caused her to lose her focus – and lose her natural performance. She regained her performance ability by going back to her younger mental state of when she was 11 years old.

QUIET THE MIND

The mind must be quiet for best concentration. A jumpy mind, a wandering mind, a distracted mind, and a cluttered mind cannot concentrate. You want to concentrate, then quiet the mind. Practice and you will learn.

HYPNOSIS

Nothing strange here. Hypnosis is nothing more than intense concentration. Everyone has been hypnotized. Sometimes while watching a movie or sporting event a person will become so focused that they may not hear someone talking to them. Sometimes you become oblivious to the world while doing some task. This is all hypnosis is. Practice concentration and focus and you can perform your skills in a state of "playing out of your mind".

THE ZONE

The zone is a state of self-hypnosis. Some may not like the word hypnosis and will swear that they did not achieve the hypnotic state, but they are wrong. The zone, self-hypnosis, intense concentration, are all similar states - a state of no distractions. These are desirable states to perform in. When a person performs "out of their mind" the expression is very accurate.

Perform with no mind, no thought, no distractions, and no nothing. Just execute.

ENTERING THE ZONE

It is very simple to describe how to enter the zone but not so easy to accomplish. It takes practice and lots of it. Fortunately it can be done. The first step in the process is to clear the mind. Let everything go. Stay in the present. Relax the mind and body. The second phase is to focus or concentrate on the task at hand and nothing else. The concentration is not on concentrating but on eliminating all distractions. The final phase is to just do it. Trust the subconscious to perform, which it will. There is no thinking and no analyzing. Just doing it. Do it and it get done? This is performing 'the nothing to do principle'.

To perform the 'just doing phase', some recommend singing a song. Singing a song helps to eliminate the conscious mind from interfering with the subconscious mind in controlling the body. It works for some.

TIGHTENING THE MIND

Bruce Lee, the famed martial artist, made this statement to Joe Hyams who wrote the book ZEN IN THE MARTIAL ARTS: "How many times have I told you both to concentrate all the energy of the body and mind on one specific target or goal at a time? The secret of *kime* (tightening of the mind) is to exclude all extraneous thoughts, thoughts that are not concerned with achieving your immediate goal. A good martial artist puts his mind on one thing at a time. He takes one thing as it comes, finishes with it and passes on to the next. Like a Zen master, he is not concerned with the past or the future, only with what he is doing at the moment. Because his mind is tight, he is calm and is able to maintain strength in reserve. And then there will be room for only one thought, which will fill his entire being as water fills a pitcher. You wasted an enormous amount of energy because you did not localize and focus your mind. Always remember: in life as well as on the mat an unfocused or 'loose' mind wastes energy."

LEARNING

NLP (Neuro-Linguistic Programming) learning is based on the involvement of the senses – visual (sight), auditory (hearing), kinesthetic (feel), olfactory (smell). In motor skill learning the main senses are visual and kinesthetic with some auditory. Youngsters learn by watching and imitating. Adults should learn this way but they tend to become so technical and analytical that they become paralyzed by analysis. Some analysis is necessary but it must not be overdone. The adult must observe and then feel the skill. This sounds easy but in reality it is not so. Feel is so deceptive with many skill learners. Golf and tennis teachers often find that their students do not really know the exact location of the racket or golf club during the skills. For example, many golf students, when told to stop their backswing at waist high, actually go well past this position. Oddly enough, it is rare to have one take the backswing short of the waist. Words do not teach feel. Experience teaches feel. The teacher or coach must provide consistent experiences to the student to learn the feel required. Since every student is different this is often difficult but not impossible. Good teachers are able to do it.

CHANGING A HABIT

Gallwey (THE INNER GAME OF TENNIS) gives an interesting analysis on changing a skill performance or skill habit.

The Usual Way of Learning is to:

1. Criticize or judge past behavior.
2. Tell yourself to change by using word commands.
3. Try hard and make yourself do it right.
4. Make critical judgments about results.

The Inner Game Way of Learning

1. Observe what is happening. Make no judgments.
2. Ask yourself to change and then program by feel and imagery.
3. Let it happen.
4. Observe results and evaluate.

The inner game way is to use imagery to direct the commands to the subconscious and then let it happen. Give it a chance. Do not press or try too hard. Evaluate results calmly and objectively. Then try again.

BODY CONTROL

If there is a secret to sports it may be in body control or body awareness. To achieve body control one must achieve mind control. Mind control does not come by talking to the body. The mind does not understand language like English or French. The mind thinks in pictures, often called imagery or visualization. The player must learn to talk to the body in picture, the language of the mind.

Research has shown that good visualization imprints the brain in the same area used for the actual physical execution. This means that visualization sets up the brain for the firing of the neurological system to activate the motor nerves to stimulate the muscles for skill execution.

LET IT LEARN

When you perform a skill you must let the body make it happen. If you do not know how to do the skill then you must let the body learn. To learn, you must let the conscious mind set the goal or target and then let the subconscious operate. It will be wild for a time, but as practice continues the subconscious learns and stores the experiences in memory. Soon there are sufficient experiences in the memory for the muscles to draw on, which is often referred to as muscle memory. Skill execution becomes learned by observation of others and by feeling the skill.

HYPNOTIC TOUCH

Alex Morrison, the well renowned golf teacher in the 30's and 40's, had a unique method in his teaching. He would explain the one thing he wanted the student to do. As the student practiced, Morrison would simply tap his student with the grip end of his golf club where the student was making the error. If the front foot was picking up instead of rolling then Alex would tap the student's foot and have the student repeat the swing. The reason for the tap was to make the student focus on the proper foot movement. The tap would create a picture in the students mind, an image of execution.

It usually took many taps for the student to achieve the objective. Also, it usually meant less talk as the student would feel the error where the tap occurred. This also prevented the student from trying to process the information verbally. The learning was now a feeling (kinesthetic) process and not so much a verbal process.

Morrison felt that the tapping practice helped the student to achieve attention. He liked the word "attention" rather than the word "concentration". Morrison felt that to some people the word concentration conveys strain, stress, tension, bulging muscles and a furrowed brow. He stresses attention; not tension. As your attention goes, so goes your whole game.

TENSION OR TIGHTNESS

Tension is considered to be the number one enemy to performance. Athletes, dancers, singers, and actors all suffer from performance tension, usually brought on by what is referred to as performance anxiety. Our body uses too many muscles and not just the required muscles for the task. When this happens, coordination is affected. When one muscle contracts, the antagonist muscle must relax. If the antagonist muscle does not relax then it will cause coordination problems.

Freeing the mind of mechanics and distractions will free the body for execution. Tension in the muscles hampers performance. A tense muscle cannot respond as accurately or as efficiently as a controlled muscle. Notice the wording is controlled muscle and not relaxed muscle. A relaxed muscle is a limp muscle. Before a muscle can perform, it has to be in a state of tonus. This means some tension in the required muscle is required for a quick response.

In skill performance, tension is usually caused by trying too hard and/or trying to be too perfect. Golfers, batters, tennis players, and bowlers, when under pressure, often have shorter back-swings and restricted movements as a result of tension in the body. The muscles are under too much tension and therefore cannot move into their required full positions. The controlled muscle will move into its correct position.

W. Timothy Gallwey (THE INNER GAME OF GOLF, Random House, NY1981) found that he could help control his tightness in golf by humming a tune. Humming freed his swing and he was able to let it happen. Humming also blocked out the possibility of distractions entering the mind. Basketball free throw shooters, bowlers, archers, etc. may find humming helpful. Richard Zokol on the PGA golf tour wore ear phones playing music while he played in tournaments. Maybe music can ease the savage beast?

Another way to help reduce tension is to tense the body to maximum tension, and then easing off or letting go of the tension, before performing the skill. Some claim that Moe Norman, the greatest ball striker to play golf, did this before his shot. Actually, this technique is not new, as yoga and Zen have taught this thousands of years ago. By going from one extreme to the other the body feels both states and is more readily able to take the desired state of relaxation.

It is unfortunate that whenever the human body is in a state of uncertainty, fear or the unknown, the muscles tends to tighten. The mind is in doubt, as it does not know what to expect. Doubt causes problems. Doubt creates too many distractions in the mind. Doubt often causes hesitations in movements. Hesitations are disastrous.

DOUBT

As previously discussed, the element of doubt is extremely disastrous to skill execution. Gallway (THE INNER GAME OF GOLF) goes so far as to claim that doubt is a more basic problem than "the much studied phenomena of anxiety, tension and fear of failure. The golfer, having doubt as to which club to use, has ruined many golf shots. Either club would have produced a fairly successful shot but the doubt element destroyed any chance of a good shot". Basketball players have had many shots blocked when they took the slight hesitation on the shot because of doubt. Hockey and soccer players have also experienced the same thing.

Overanalyzing and out-thinking yourself creates doubt. Doubt comes from not trusting your ability and letting the conscious take over. Doubt lets distractions enter the mind and prevents the clear mind, the single focus.

When doubt creeps into the psych of many players, there is an attempt to try harder. As we already know this will generally not produce successful results. Players who feel the stress of doubt, must make their mind certain. Right or wrong, the certain mind is better than the doubtful mind. The certain mind is confident. The certain mind trusts the subconscious of the body to let it happen. When performing, be certain, be confident, trust yourself and then let it go.

EXPERIENCED LEARNING

Physical skill learning is by experience, not by words. Experience is gained by practice, correct and accurate practice. We learned to walk through experience not by listening to our parents telling us how to move the body and how to balance. We fell a lot, but it was part of the learning process. When learning to walk, it is a good thing that you are too young to understand your parents' commands. Body awareness, feel, and balance have to be experienced. Words cannot teach you these critical factors for skill execution.

UPTIGHT

The center of gravity governs balance. This center of gravity is a point located two inches above the belly button but in the center of the body. In the martial arts this point is called ‘chi’ or ‘ki’ and must stay centered with the body throughout the execution of the skill. When a player becomes anxious, nervous, or tries too hard they often “leave their center” and go off balance. Sometimes the balance problem may only be slight, but that is enough. Notice how the great players are always in balance throughout the entire skill execution. Lose balance, and you lose accuracy and power. Loss of balance is such a serious problem that players are often injured when off balance. In fact, the number of injuries caused by loss of balance is quite high. Muscle pulls are often the result of a balance problem.

The balance factor is so crucial, that balance should be the first thing studied when trying to correct a skill execution problem.

SLOW MOTION

Performing a skill in slow motion can be effective in learning. The teachings of Zen and other Far East philosophies emphasize this in almost all their skill learning. Westerners are now accepting this into their teachings of golf, tennis, baseball, basketball, and other sports. The muscles learn the correct movement when moving slowly as there is less chance of a mistake. As the movement is learned, the moves become faster. Soon the optimum is reached.

Slow motion is an excellent means of practicing a skill. Most skills happen so fast that the learner's mind cannot catch up to the body movements. Also, many learners are trying to achieve too much power and naturally go out of balance. Zen and the Martial Arts use slow motion skill execution to many of their skill. Going slow gives the mind and the body time to feel the muscular movements of the skill. Neurological pathways then have a chance to be set accurately. As feel increases and understanding of the skill gets better then the player can slowly increase the speed of the skill. In time, with practice, the maximum speed will be achieved for the skill.

BREAKING HABITS

Breaking a habit, especially a bad habit, is often difficult. Quite often the habit seems to be broken, only to reappear under pressure conditions. Perhaps the best way to break a bad habit is not to break it, just create a new habit. When needed just do the new habit. Let the old habit fade away under its own lack of use.

TAKING A LESSON

Many players do not know how to take a lesson. Some players come to the lesson with preconceived ideas and notions. Some players come to the lesson to try and impress the teacher with their knowledge. Some players come to the lesson and are afraid to try new things or to experiment. Some players come to the lesson because it is the 'in' thing to do. Some actually come to a lesson to get better but will not put in the time to practice after the lesson. Sometimes, only a few will take the lesson and actually practice diligently to get better. Practice, over time, will let the lesson sink into the mind and body.

When you take a lesson, you must do what the instructor wants you to do. You may not believe in the move or even feel you can do it, but you must try. If it does not work, then the instructor will know more about your capabilities. Give your teacher a chance. Sometimes, actually many times, the move the instructor wants you to perform does work out for the best. Give it a chance.

LEARNING IS FUN

The authors recall an interview with a coach on why some players are better than others. The real answer lies in everything from genes and genetics to attitude, effort and practice, but the coach's answer has merit. He claimed that the great ones loved to practice and learn. At practice time they learned. They had fun. Learning was fun. They stayed after practice time to 'horse-around', to play, to get better and to have fun.

Albert A. Michelson was the first person in the United States to win a Nobel Prize. His life was devoted to the study of the speed of light. When asked why he devoted so much time and life to this study replied, "It was so much fun". (From the book FLOW). This is the flow experience. It happens in sports, work and life. When athletes look back on their careers they also say, "It was so much fun."

NOTHING TO DO PRINCIPLE

Behrens has the "nothing to do principle" for his students. He shoots an arrow into a paper cup and claims that he did not really do anything. The arrow was in the cup before the release. He visualizes the arrow in the cup before the release. There was "nothing to do" as it was already done. This principle means to visualize the target and let the action happen. In golf it is the ball dropping in the hole. In basketball it is the ball dropping in the basket. In bowling it is the ball in the pocket. The mind sees the end result. No thought of mechanics or distractions. The mind is clear. The body does "nothing". It just happens.

Eugen Herrigel, in his fascinating book ZEN IN THE ART OF ARCHERY (Vintage Books, NY 1971) talks of the "nothing to do principle" in archery. For years he worked on this principle until he was capable of letting it happen. He writes, "Only after considerable time did more right shots occasionally come off, which the Master signalized by a deep bow. How it happened that they loosed themselves without my doing anything". In many sports, performed while in the zone, the performer cannot explain how it happened. It just did. Many golfers, when they hit that great shot, claim they do not know how it happened. In fact they often say that they just hung on to the club. The club swung them. They did not swing the club.

DETACHMENT

In the learning process the player must eventually reach the stage of detachment. The player must detach himself from ego, fear of failure, results and the incident or skill. The player simply must let go. This is not easy, but the great ones accomplish it.

When beginners learn, they start off full of confidence, fearless and courageous. They are attached to the skill. They feel they must control everything. They must feel that it is them that makes the skill accomplished. They cannot detach themselves and let it happen. When they let it happen, they feel it is out of their control, and they are not controlling the skill. Ironically, this is what they must do to control the situation. This is what they must learn. This is difficult. Practice will teach and learn.

The real beginners do not understand all the complexities of the sport skill involved. As their learning progresses, they feel more useless and become disappointed with their progress. Their expectations are rushed. In time, they will understand the real learning of the mental aspects and the feel of the skill takes time. Improvement is inevitable.

It is interesting to note that all great athletes at one time or another have thought of giving up their sport as they felt they were not making any progress and not getting better. The reason they felt they were not getting better was because of their expectations. Their expectations were progressing faster than their ability. The more they learned about their skill the more they understood the complexity. The more they understood, the more they realized they were not reaching the level they expected. At this stage of development the great ones kept going and finally they did reach the new level. They were able to let go, to free up the body and mind, to make the complex simple.

"If you are not concerned about the outcome of a circumstance, you will experience no fear. When you attach yourself to expectations, anxiety and fear will overcome you. The outcome will be what it will be, regardless of your expectations and fears." (THICK FACE, BLACK HEART by Chin-Ning Chu. Warner Books, NY 1992).

THE OUTCOME

"For my best performances I'm thinking about how to shoot correctly (form); letting shooting sequences run through my head. . . seeing myself in control, confident. It is very important for me not to start adding the score and projecting what the score might be. If during the last few ends I become nervous and start to worry about blowing it, I have to work hard to keep my shooting sequence in mind (form, form, form) and not the glory of shooting a high score." (IN PURSUIT OF EXCELLENCE by Terry Orlick).

EMPTY MIND

"For my best performances, I empty my mind and I feel as though it isn't me performing, but at the same time I feel totally connected with the feelings in my body. It's as if my subconscious is doing the performance. I imagine the perfect movement in my head and the rest follows automatically." (IN PURSUIT OF EXCELLENCE by Terry Orlick)

THE TEACHER'S DUTY

"The instructor's business is not to show the way itself, but to enable the pupil to get the feel of this way to the goal by adapting it to his individual peculiarities". ZEN IN THE ART OF ARCHERY by Eugen Herrigel. Vintage Books, NY, 1971.

THE SENSES

In skill learning, we rely too much on the sense of vision. Vision can and is helpful, and is necessary for some skills, but the other senses must be brought into play. The kinesthetic sense must accompany vision with equal importance. The sense of sound is also important. All striking sports love the sound of contact. The sound of contact carries a message. We are familiar with the message from the contact of bat and ball, of pool cue and cue ball, of tennis racket and tennis ball, and golf club and golf ball. We learn to recognize the sound of the sweet spot contact and the missed sweet spot contact. Learn to read it. Develop your senses for all skills. Practice. Practice. Practice.

BEGINNERS MIND

"The mind of an infant is empty; it is fresh. It has no preconceived ideas; it sees things as they are. It is free from the habits of experience and therefore open to all possibilities. The infant has no thoughts of achievement, and makes no demands. It makes no judgments, no distinctions. The infant lives in the absolute present". (THE BOOK OF FIVE RINGS).

Coaches and players should open up their minds more often. So many coaches are so stereotyped in their philosophy. The say they are open to new ideas but not really. They are scared to try new things and are afraid to experiment. Coaches, with the beginners mind, know how to take the old and the new. They keep looking for new and better ways. They experiment. They take a chance. If the idea is well thought-out and well rehearsed then it has a good chance for success. The risk is minimal. He who dares - wins.

TRAINING TO FORGET

This seems like a contradiction, but it is not. We train to learn, but once we learned the skill, we do not think about it. We perform it. We learn it and then we forget it, as it will respond when we need it. Goaltenders in hockey and soccer learn the skill of stopping the puck or ball when they let it happen. The goaltenders wait until the shooter makes the first move, then they react. Simple, but often difficult. When a player wants to "deke" or deceive an opponent they let the opponent move first. On a confrontation, the person who makes the first move usually gets deceived. Samurai swordsmen in ancient Japan would study their opponent and let them make the first move with the sword. If the opponent made the first move it was his last move. Like the modern day athlete, the samurai learned his skills and then used the one needed for the situation. The samurai and athlete did not plan their moves beforehand. They just let it happen.

Myamoto Musashi, the Samurai, in his THE BOOK OF FIVE RINGS, explains the process quite well. "Think of any activity that you perform that you are good at. It can be investment banking, cooking, tennis, speechmaking, organizing, or anything. What is it that makes you good at it? Is it your training, or the tools you use? Or is it the experience you have accumulated in doing it? It is all of these things, in varying degrees, but the missing element is the crucial one. Your attitude, your approach, the sense of confidence and the purpose (no hesitation) you bring to your activity are what people observe when they say you are "good at it."

Zen is a practice for life; in Zen, first comes the technique, practiced so many times that it is forgotten. Then you begin to use it. It is when you do not think about it anymore that you do it so well. Zen is no more than that. But it is reaching the state that the training is all about. The professional dancer who makes it look easy has trained constantly and endured great pain. The tennis pro who flies around the court, making impossible shots, does so, not because of any superhuman qualities, but because he has practiced and practiced, as the dancer has, until the movements are internalized. There is no longer any conscious direction in the movement. When you marvel at the way someone whips up a dinner for ten on short notice, or the way someone makes an impromptu speech, you are marveling at the same thing – the approach, the confidence, the naturalness of the behavior. There is no time to prepare, no time to think, no time to hesitate. There you are. Zen.

As was said earlier, first the technique is practiced so often that it is internalized and "forgotten", and then one learns to use it. Mastering the technique is mind over body; discipline, hard work, forcing the body to accept the rules and pain and the utter exhaustion of constant practice, until the body learns. Using the technique is body over mind; the body just does what it knows."

This last paragraph is interesting as it tells of how the mind is over the body, controlling the body. Once the skill is learned then the body is over the mind as there is no thought process, no signals from the mind. The body just responds as it knows how, as it was taught and learned. It is almost as if the body or muscles have their own mind. It is a programmed response, much like hitting the enter key on the computer to execute the program.

PSYCHOLOGICAL AND PHYSICAL REACTIONS

When stress appears, the mind goes into psychological reactions of fear, anxiety, panic, confusion, doubt and uncertainty and physical reactions of sweating, trembling, nausea, weakness and shaky with uncoordinated movements. It is even possible that the above reactions may cause temporary paralysis. If these reactions are prevalent in a sporting situation then performance will be detrimental.

STRESS

Mihaly Csikszenthihaly explains how to cope with stress. He claims that some people are weakened by stress while others become stronger with stress. Those who are successful in coping with stress are able to transform a hopeless situation into a flow experience. This is achieved through three steps.

1. **Self-assurance**. Richard Logan (THE FLOW EXPERIENCE IN SOLITARY ORDEALS in the JOURNAL OF HUMANISTIC PSYCHOLOGY 25(4):79-89) found that people who survived severe physical ordeals had an attitude that destiny was in their hands. They determined their own fate despite the environment. They were self-assured and not self-centered.

2. **The enviroment**. In stressful situations these people thoroughly study their surroundings and environment. They spend very little time thinking about themselves. They are in harmony with their environment and thus have a chance for coping with it. Understanding the environment leads to a strategy for adapting and coping with the situation.

3. **New solutions**. The mind works to create new solutions and different approaches to the situation. This is the use of the beginner's mind which is discussed elsewhere in this book. The mind is open.

Coaches, athletes and non-athletes, all deal with stress. Practices and games must develop these three concepts. Too many coaches and athletes just go about their drills in with the expectations that this sufficient to provide performance in game and pressure situations. It is not that easy. Drills and practice must be designed and performed to game or match like conditions with as much pressure as possible. Drills alone do not necessarily transfer into game conditions. Practice must be under game conditions.

RHYTHM

Pace, flow and rhythm are important factors in skill execution. When a player has the technique learned, then if problems occur, it is often a result of problems with rhythm. Work on the skill's rhythm and the execution of a skill often returns. Teams, and not just individuals, must work on team rhythm. The flow and timing of the team has everyone working together. It is one machine, one being, composed of individuals. Although golf is considered an individual sport, there are many times it is a team sport.

HEIHO

Heiho means the path or the way to enlightment. Miyamoto Musashi (BOOK OF FIVE RINGS) says, "Your mastery of Heiho cannot be considered firm unless you understand the rhythm with which you can avoid being drawn into the rhythm of the opponent. Victory is achieved in the Heiho of conflict, by ascertaining the rhythm of each opponent, by attacking with a rhythm not anticipated by the opponent, and by the use of knowledge of the rhythm of the abstract."

When playing you must not let yourself fall into the rhythm and pattern of your opponent. If this happens, then the opposition controls you. You must control the opposition. Fight to control the rhythm of the match. Control the rhythm and you control the match. Control of the match's rhythm may come quickly or it may take almost the entire match. Whatever, don't give up. Many games and matches have been won when control was not achieved until the dying minutes of the contest. "Don't give up. Don't ever give up." Jim Valvono, the basketball coach at North Carolina State, on his fight with cancer.

To establish the rhythm, it may be helpful to think like the opposition. When you understand the opposition, then you can control the opposition. If you do not understand the opposition then trying to control them is a hit and miss strategy. Scouting opponents and teams can help. Learn to read the opposition while the contest is in progress. When playing, the good athlete reads the opposition as well as his own performance. Strategy is useless if it does not apply to the situation, the opposition and yourself.

SELF TALK

Talking to yourself can be good and it can be bad. You can be critical of yourself but you must be careful that you do not berate yourself or get too down on yourself. It is ironic, but we can say things to ourselves that we would not accept from someone else. The best self-talk is positive self-talk. You can get mad at yourself, but get mad in a positive way. Some are able to get more energy with positive self-talk. Do not let self-talk become a distraction to your performance.

THE DANCE

Fred Roche, in the ZEN OF RUNNING (Random House, NY 1975): “If the dance of the run isn’t fun then discover another dance, because without fun, the good of the run is undone, and a suffering runner always quits, sooner or later.” Take this quote and substitute any sport because the philosophy is the same. We see it all the time.

SHAPING

Karen Pryor in her book DON'T SHOOT THE DOG (Bantam Books, NY 1985) talks about how to use reinforcement and shaping in training animals. The book is very interesting and many of her ideas are useable in learning sport skills. The key to reinforcing learning is to reinforce the behavior until it is learned and then gradually wean off the reinforcing as the habit becomes established.

The following are excerpts from her 10 laws on shaping. According to Pryor, shaping "consists of taking a very small tendency in the right direction and shifting it, one small step at a time, toward an ultimate goal." To her this applies to coaching sports.

1. <u>Raise criteria in increments small enough so that the subject always has a realistic chance for reinforcement.</u> Raising the criteria slowly gives the learning a chance to become ingrained into the body. Move too fast and previous learning is not strong enough to give a good base for future learning. Unless the learning is strong it will fall apart under pressure. Build a good base for advanced learning.

2. Train one thing at a time. Don't try to shape for two criteria simultaneously. This is a good one. So many times we work on too many things at once. Golf lessons often go this way. One lesson and the students say, "There are so many things to know". Well, at this stage the student was taught to do too many things at once. Confusion becomes the norm. Coaches must remember they are teachers. They are not there to impress the students with their knowledge. Coaches are teachers – so teach for your students to learn.

Pryor says that one reinforcement cannot convey two pieces of information. It is like learning to putt in golf. Shape for distance and then shape for direction, or visa-versa, but learn one then the other. After both are learned, then combine them. This is quicker and better. Very often when we are learning a skill and we find ourselves stuck without improvement, it is because we are trying to improve two or more things at once.

3. Always put the current level of response into a variable schedule of reinforcement before adding or raising criteria. Once a behavior or skill is learned, then the variable schedule of reinforcement is applied. This means that once behavior is learned, the reinforcement is

gradually weaned away to be used occasionally.

4. When introducing a new criterion, temporarily relax the old ones. In golf, racquetball, tennis, and other striking skills you need to work on speed of the swing until you get it down. Then you work on aim or direction. If you find direction of the ball all over the place, it is because you trying two things at once. Relax or forget the speed factor and continue to swing hard but focus on the aim only. Gradually the aim will come around. It is a trusting thing.

5. Stay ahead of your subject. Coaches must stay ahead of their players in case the learning is moving faster than the coach expected. Good coaches do this by their planning.

6. Don't change trainers in midstream. Pryor feels that coaching should not be changed unless the students are not learning. If no learning is happening then there is nothing to lose in making a change. Students or players get used to the techniques of their coach. Change coaches and the players have to relearn some things.

7. If one shaping procedure is not eliciting progress, try another. Every coach should know this one. Too many coaches blame the players when learning is not taking place. Sometimes it is the coach's fault in not teaching through a different technique. If it is not working – try another method.

8. Don't interrupt a training session. This is an important one. When coaching or teaching, do the job and do not leave the situation to answer a phone or talk to a non-player. The players need your full attention during the training session. Besides, if you leave the players they will think they are not important. Sometimes such a break in the training session causes the session to lose momentum and interest.

9. if a learned behavior deteriorates, review your shaping. This is the old adage of "back to fundamentals." Remember it. It works.

10. Quit while you are ahead. This procedure leaves the player(s) with a feeling of accomplishment. The last behavior is the one most remembered. Sometimes if the training goes on too long, the good responses are lost and the skill level deteriorates. This can lead to frustration and lack of confidence.

MEDITATION

Meditation can be helpful in learning to concentrate and relax. Actually many athletes use meditation and don't realize it. These athletes usually sit quietly before a game, or match, in order to clear their mind and relax their body. Sometimes, they concentrate and visualize on what they plan to do and how to perform. It is much like visualization except formal meditation focuses on one item or no items while visualization may focus on the many skills involved in the performance. Either way, the procedure is helpful. The great ones do it.

LEARN LIKE A CHILD

Dan Millman has written several books on the inner athlete and inner life. His discovery to this style of learning came from watching his little daughter at play. He was trying to understand how children learn at a much faster and easier pace than adults. His daughter was playing with the cat on the floor. The daughter was relaxed and mindless like the cat. Then it struck him. Talent is not so much the presence of certain talents but rather the absence of mental, physical and emotional obstructions - qualities that adults often lack when trying to learn.

DEMANDS

Physical training makes demands on the body. If the demands are progressive and gradual, the body will adapt to these demands. If the demands are too demanding and not in gradual increments, the body becomes over-taxed and breaks down. This is the principle of overload. The law of overloads works well if the overload is trained properly.

Mental training makes demands on the mind. If the demands are progressive and gradual, the mind will adapt to these demands. If the demands are too demanding and not in a gradual increment, the mind becomes over-taxed, overloaded and breaks down. This is the principle of overload; the same principle that is used for the body. Good coaches and athletes know how to use both the body and the mind in their training sessions. Too often coaches just train the body and tell the players to use the mind, or think, or concentrate. This does not work. The mind must be trained. The mind, like the body, can only do what it has learned to do. Coaches: never forget this law. If your player(s) fail to do something in a game or match then check for reasons. Be honest because it just might be your fault in not having taught the skill or mind set. Athletes often take the blame for poor coaching.

We learn to meet the demands of growing. This is a law of life, not just sports. The demands increase as we gain experience. Mistakes occur, but mistakes are not the problem. Failure to learn from our mistakes is the problem.

SLOW DOWN

An experiment by sport psychologists Robert Weinberg and Daniel Gould showed an interesting twist to the 110% effort. They had runners run at a 110% effort, for an all out effort. A few days later the same runners ran the same race but were asked to run at 95% of their maximum effort. The results were surprising. The 95% effort produced better results. Logically this seems incorrect, as the stronger effort should achieve better results. Actually, their reasoning is simple and based on the laws of coordination. Muscles can only contract, so when one muscle is contracting, the antagonist muscle must relax. The better this relaxing and contracting is accomplished the better the coordination. By doing an all out effort of 110% the speed of the movement causes a timing problem in the relaxing and contracting of the muscles. This means that the muscle and the antagonist muscle may be both contracting at a fraction of the moment. When both muscles are contracting one muscle is working against the other muscle. (PLAY SLOW MOTION GOLF FOR BETTER RESULTS by Tom Dorsel in Golf Illustrated, Jan/Feb 2001)

This occurrence is common with golfers. They take a nice and effective practice swing at less than maximum effort and then look like gorillas when they try to swing very hard at the golf ball. Their muscles are tight and uncoordinated. Top golf pros swing at 80 to 90% of their maximum. Basketball, soccer, and hockey players pace themselves in the same manner. Good athletes pace themselves to 80 to 90%. The slap shot in hockey is in the same category. Soccer players shooting on goal fall into this category.

Dorsel talks about Steve Thomas, a long drive champion, who was asked to swing as hard as he could at a golf ball so they could measure his swing speed. He was recorded at 102mph. Next he was asked to take his normal swing. His swing speed was 167mph. His normal swing was actually 65mph faster, a result of better muscular coordination by being better able to control the skill.

Slowing down the skill is difficult because we feel that if we slow down our movements we will not achieve our best results. As you can see this is a myth. We only slow down a little, just a little short of maximum for better timing and control. It must be remembered that slowing down is a mental skill as well as a physical skill. When the pressure is on, and we are highly motivated, our thinking speeds up and we often get ahead of ourselves. We walk faster, we talk faster, we breathe faster and naturally this leads to performing our skill faster – to the disastrous 110% effort.

Slowing down requires practice. These steps can help.

1. Be able to recognize the factors of the racing mind and body. When you can recognize these factors like breathing, heartbeat, etc., you will be able to take action.

2. Slow down your thinking, breathing, etc. Get your mind under control. Do not let yourself panic. Have no fear. Visualize your slower motions. Remember you are only slowing down just a little below maximum.

The Master Martial Artist, Bruce Lee, has often said that less effort means faster and more powerful moves.

MASTERY

George Leonard is an aikido master and has written many books that are helpful to coaches. One of his excellent books is the ULTIMATE ATHLETE. Well worth reading.

In the book MASTERY (Plume Book, NY 1992) George Leonard gives five steps to mastery or mastering a skill. They are as follows.

1. Instruction. Mastery requires first rate instruction.

2. Practice. The top athletes love to practice. It is more than just getting better. They are able to practice a lot because they just love it. A research study was done to find out why some athletes were better than others and what separated the good ones from the poorer ones. The only conclusion they found was that the good ones loved to practice, practice and practice. George claims "The master of any game is generally a master of practice.

3. Surrender. This means surrendering to your teacher and to the demands of your discipline. You must be willing to make the changes necessary and not resist the new ways. The students must be willing to give up their beliefs and rigid attitudes. The students are not experts, they are learners. Because they are

learning, and not experts, they are called students.

4. Intentionality. The power of the mental game. The use of visualization/imagery.

5. The edge. "Almost without exception, those we know as masters are dedicated to the fundamentals of their calling. They are zealots of practice, connoisseurs of the small incremental step." They "are precisely the ones who are likely to challenge previous limits, to take risks for the sake of higher performance, and even to become obsessive at times in that pursuit." It is a fine edge between the endless, goalless practice and the alluring goals.

PERFORMING

RHYTHM

The rhythm or pace of a skill is extremely important. In fact, most slumps by athletes are simply a result of rhythm problems. Once the body has learned the skill, then the movements are there. They just need to be put into the proper timing or rhythm. When things go bad, the first thing to work on is rhythm, pace, and timing.

Roger Bannister, in his book BREAKING THE FOUR MINUTE MILE said, "The earth seemed to move with me . . . a fresh rhythm entered my body. No longer conscious of my movement I discovered a new unity with nature . . . a new source of power and beauty, a source I never knew existed."

TWO GAMES

All sports have two games – one is the actual game, or external game, and the other is the inner game, or mental game. Both are important. The mental game is nothing if the physical game is weak. The physical game needs the mental game for maximum efficiency. Both must be practiced. Many coaches like to say how important the mental game is but few actually teach and practice it.

THE GAME IS WITH YOURSELF

All sports are against yourself. It is not about winning or losing. It is about doing your best. Playing to your potential. Overcoming your fears and distractions. After all, if you cannot achieve these goals then winning is difficult. What value is there to winning against inferior competition? There is no testing of the self.

Chungliang Al Huang and Jerry Lynch in their book THINKING BODY, DANCING MIND (Bantam Books, NY 1992) explain the game within yourself in the following quotation. "The Western approach to athletics emphasizes aggression, with the athlete as a combatant and the game a battle. For the Tao Athlete, however, assertiveness replaces aggression and the physical game becomes the arena for the ongoing development of internal, psychological strengths. Tao Athletes work to recognize and overcome 'inner demons' that hinder their concentration and performance, all the self-imposed obstacles and limitations that they may have unconsciously erected."

Good players use sport as a source of developing their minds for better performances. The game to such players is a battle of the body and the mind. Sport is a source of development. The better ones develop better. They eventually win, but winning is not the main goal. Winning happens with development. Studies have confirmed that most athletes are more concerned about their individual or team's performance than winning. They know they will win if they perform as desired. Steve Prefontaine used to say that he could run his best and lose and run his worst and win, so why is winning so important. Doing my best is important. He knew a secret to winning.

TRYING TOO HARD

Tim Gallwey in his book THE INNER GAME OF TENNIS (Random House, NY 1974) describes how he found the Zen "effortless effort" in the paradox of "trying too hard." Tim had a student who continually hit the frame of her racket instead of the racquet strings. To verify this problem he had her hit 10 forehand strokes. She hit only two balls off the center of the racket strings. The next step was to have her concentrate real hard on the focus of the center of the racket. This resulted in four hits on the center. The next round of hits Tim had her focus on the spin of the ball with the mind on the seams of the tennis ball without thinking about contact, just to focus on the spin and let the racket go by itself. The student then hit nine out of ten balls on the strings. The one miss was the result of losing the focus on the spin.

By not focusing on how to hit the ball, the student was able to relax and respond to the situation more alertly. She was into "effortless effort". Golfers have often said that when they hit that outstanding shot they cannot explain how they did it. It just happened. It was effortless. Baseball and softball players have made the same comments after the big hit.

PARADOXICAL INTERVENTION

This is an interesting technique to correct a mistake or a flaw in one's skill execution. Typing teachers do this when their students make mistakes typing. They have the student type the mistake several times until the mistake becomes understood. Hard to imagine but it does work. Paradoxical intervention is also used in the sport world. A psychologist, Bud A. McClure Ph.D., explains this in his golf article in GOLF TIPS (April 1998 p.101). To cure a slice, have the student practice the slice. With practice the student learns and understands the mistakes more fully. The following well explained quote is from his article.

"Exaggerating, or overdoing the flaw, is important. Many bad shots are the result of fractional miss-hits caused by slight swing mistakes that are very difficult to discern. So by exaggerating a flaw, you magnify your perception of it, making it easier for you to learn how to do the opposite – like turning a slice into a draw. And that is how a mistake can be beautiful: by learning to do it well, you also teach yourself how not to do it. So don't be afraid of your mistakes. Instead welcome them, practice them, and exaggerate them. By doing that, you'll be able to eliminate them."

Some feel the best way to learn to hit a straight ball is to learn to slice and hook first. Once these are learned it is easy to understand the mechanics of the straight ball.

HONOR YOUR OPPONENT BY GIVING YOUR BEST

Honor your opponent by giving your best is a Zen philosophy. Every athlete and recreational player should adopt this philosophy. When playing you do your best so that you make your opponent work harder and better. When an opponent does not try, then it is not much fun playing. We have all experienced this at one time or another. When one does not try, then they have a ready-made excuse if they lose or did not play well. These people are more concerned about their ego or self-image than they are in performing well. These people are usually quitters or losers. When self-image or ego is on the line then performance suffers.

PLAYING BAD / PLAYING GOOD

Playing bad is the result of physical and/or mental problems. Physical problems are readily noticeable. Fatigue, injury, and lack of technique, and lack of finesse are some of the physical problems. The mental problems are not so easily noticed, but usually break down into too much instruction, too much self-judgment or too much self-criticism. Judgment and criticism of the self is a form of too much instruction, a negative instructional format. When you tell yourself "don't do …" or "why did I do this stupid …" you are actually doing a form of instruction. Here again we are dealing with verbal instructions – not good. The other reasons for playing bad are doubt and fear of failure.

When playing good, the players almost always agree that they were relaxed, clear of mind, and gave themselves no instructions or critiques. They played with confidence. They were in the zone.

JUST DO IT

"Perfection in the art of swordsmanship is reached, according to Takuan, when the heart is troubled by no more thought of I and You, of the opponent and his sword, of one's own sword and how to wield it – no more thought of even life or death. All is emptiness: your own self, the flashing sword, and the arms that wield it. Even the thought of emptiness is no longer there." From this absolute emptiness, states Takuan, "comes the most wondrous unfoldment of doing.

This quote does not need elaboration. Just understand it. (ZEN IN THE ART OF ARCHERY by Eugen Herrigel. Vintage Press, NY 1971)

SLUMPS

Slumps are common to athletes. Everyone usually gets them at one time or another. Slumps are usually caused be trying too hard, seeking too much perfection, thinking too much and expecting too much. When in a slump, many athletes escalate these problems and the slump gets worse. Very often, the best way to handle a slump is to stop worrying about it. Worry escalates the problem. Relax. Enjoy the game. Don't force the situation. The percentages gradually fall back into place.

FATIGUE

Fatigue is a physiological process where the body becomes tired. This is natural. If you have been going all out, then you should reach a state of fatigue. Many times the problem is not the physical fatigue but the mental problems that come with it. Fatigue causes our minds to react slower, too miss a play, to be hesitant, and many other mental factors. In ice hockey a coach can tell if his players need to be changed quickly by their mental errors; a bad pass, not hanging on to the pass, or other mental errors. When these types mental errors appear in play, then the coach has to substitute the player. In sports or activities where there is no substitution, like golf, archery, and running, the players must be alert for their mental errors. The mind must not be distracted by fatigue. Fatigue is a distraction.

PERFECTIONISM

Perfectionism can become an obsession of destruction. Although it is good to have some striving for perfectionism, some athletes are so concerned about perfectionism that they lose their focus on execution. They become entailed with technique and detail. They lose their feel. Their mind becomes cluttered. Golfers often become so analytical that they lose their feel for the swing. Their fine touch leaves them.

Very often the search for perfectionism leads to depression or a self-defeating attitude. The players begin to feel that they are a failure. When they believe they are a failure, then it is difficult for them to turn it around. It can be done. Be as good as you can but let perfectionism take care of itself. You may come close but never perfect.

PASSION and OBSESSION

Great athletes have a passion for their sport. They are close to the line of obsession but do not cross-over to the obsessed. Obsession distorts one's view. Obsession alters thinking. Obsession interferes with one's reasoning. Obsession leads to disaster.

DETACHMENT

The athlete must detach themselves from the game and the outcome. Play the game and let the outcome happen. Chungliang Al Huang and Jerry Lynch explain the detachment very well. They asked athletes who were struggling with their performance how often they have had fun while playing. Most commented that they cannot remember their last enjoyable game. They feel this is ironic because fun was the reason for playing the game. They feel that the reason they cannot remember is because they cannot detach themselves from the game and the outcome. "Their emotional involvement reduces the level of joy they can experience in their sport. They lose awareness of the dance of the game. When you become attached to playing better and winning more, you push, force, or try harder. This creates anxiety, tension, and pressure; the result is less fun, less joy, and less fulfillment, coupled with sub-par performance."

Eugen Herrigel, in ZEN IN THE ART OF ARCHERY says that the pupil must become purposeless and egoless. He must be taught to be detached not only from his opponent but also from himself.

FLOW

Mihaly Csikszentmihaly, a psychologist at the University of Chicago, has become the expert on the state of flow. Entering the state of flow is emotional intelligence at its best. It is the harnessing of emotions for performance and learning. It is the state of complete absorption on the task at hand. Intense concentration is required to enter the state of flow. Focus and calmness prevail. Flow is achieved when the task at hand is usually slightly above the player's normal ability. If the task is too much above their ability, the performer will become anxious, nervous and have other negative traits. If the task is too easy, the performer becomes bored and disinterested.

In the state of flow, the difficult looks easy. Peak performance is easy. The brain is cool and calm. The brain quiets down and does not race around with thoughts or ideas. The brain lessens in cortical arousal. This lessening is the opposite to what one may think, as the demands of the task increase the brain's cortical arousal actually lessens rather than increases. The key to flow occurs when the demands are slightly above normal and the skills are well learned and the neurological pathways are well established.

Csikszentmihaly did a study with 200 artists 18 years after they finished art school. He found that the students who were in art school for the joy of painting went on to become serious painters. The other painters, who went to the school for possible future fame and wealth, drifted on to other jobs. His conclusions from the study also apply to athletes. “Painters must want to paint above all else. If the artist in front of the canvas begins to wonder how much it will sell for, or what the critics will think of it, he won’t be able to pursue original avenues. Creative achievements depend on single-minded immersion.” (FLOW: THE PSYCHOLOGY OF OPTIMAL EXPERIENCES by Mihaly Csikszentmihalyi. Harper and Row, NY 1990)

TRYING

Dan Millman gives one of the best explanations of trying and its problems. “Athletes commonly resist the natural process by *trying*. The word ‘try’ itself implies a weakness in the face of challenge. The moment we try, we are already tense; trying therefore, is a primary cause of error. In more natural actions, we omit to try. We simply walk to the refrigerator, write a letter, or water the flowers; we don’t have to try to do these things, and we perform them easily and naturally. But when faced with something we consider an imposing challenge – when self-doubt arises – we begin to try".

When competitors feel they are under pressure and begin to try, they often fall apart. Chuang Tzu, a Chinese sage, observed that "when an archer is shooting for enjoyment, he has all his skill; when he shoot for a brass buckle, he gets nervous; when he shoots for a prize of gold, he begins to see two targets."

Trying is an interesting phenomenon. When golfers try to keep the left arm straight in the backswing they tense the biceps (agonist muscle) and the triceps (antagonist muscle). When both muscles are tense we have no coordination. They are trying too hard. Basketball players, when trying to sink the free throw, will do the same thing with their arm muscles. Both athletes have lost the play instinct of the child, as Dan Millman stated earlier, when watching his daughter play with the absence of mental, physical and emotional obstructions.

GETTING WORSE

This is an interesting phenomenon as almost every athlete or competitor has gone through this stage. The athlete assumes they are getting worse. They are not improving. The college athlete feels they were better in high school, or the pro feels they were better in college. Very often they have actually improved, and are much better, even though they do not realize it. The reason for this failure attitude is that the athlete has set new standards. They have learned more about their skills in body and in mind. They have set new higher standards of their ability and have just not reached it YET. Naturally this leads to discouragement. The athlete's inner motivation must take hold. The athlete must not quit, as so many do, at this stage. Perseverance must prevail. Gradually the new standard will be met. The goal will be reached. The athlete now performs at a new level.

If one looks at the pro golf tour, as well as other sports, one will see so many athletes that have gone through this turmoil stage. Time and time again, we see tournament winners during their interview say how they were so discouraged a while back that they almost gave up the game. But, they did not give up.

Millman give an excellent view of this perspective. "And remember – sometimes when you seem to be vegetating, going nowhere, even slipping backward, you may just be backing up to get a running start."

OPPOSITION DICTATES

"As you will discover, the primary philosophical point of HEIHO is that all things are dependent upon other things." (THE BOOK OF FIVE RINGS by Myamoto Musashi. Bantam Books, NY 1982). This quote is so simple and yet so often forgotten. In sports, all attacks and counter attacks are dependent on something else. So many players and coaches say they are going to do this or do that. Such strategy may work, if you're lucky, or may not work. The opposition should govern your moves or plans. You may want to do this/that but if the opposition does something you did not plan on then you better have a backup plan. All strategy is governed by the opposition, the weather, the environment, or whatever. The weather is so often a criteria for strategy adjustments. Good athletes and good teams adjust to the situation. Never forget Murphy's Law.

NERVES BEFORE GAME

'Game nerves' are common. If the pre-game nerves start too soon and too intense, then the athlete may be drained by game time. Some nerves are good as it indicates excitement and readiness. In most cases the nerves are gone by game time. The problem is when the nerves carry over into the game.

Studies by Fenz & Epstein and Fenz & Jones showed how the pre-competition nerves affect athletes. They studied parachutists and found that prior to their jump all the parachutists' experienced increased heart rates which signified an increase in nerves. However, just prior to jump time the experienced and the good parachutist's heart rates went down while the inexperienced and poor jumpers' heart rates continued to rise. These studies indicate that all athletes get nerves, but the good ones learn to control their nerves. The poor ones cannot cope. (IN SPORT PSYCHOLOGY, AN ANALYSIS OF ATHLETE BEHAVIOR, edited by W.F. Straub, Movement Publications 1980).

EYE SHIFT

Dr. Craig Farnsworth in his book SEE IT AND SINK IT (Harper Collins Publishers, NY 1997) talks about the Laser Eye Shift. College students, to eliminate "test anxieties", as well as athletes and non-athletes when coping with stressful situations use the laser eye shift. The technique is very simple. With the head pointing straight ahead, pick out an object to the left of your straight-ahead vision. Then pick out an object to the right. Try to put some distance between the two objects. While looking straight ahead shift the eyes back and forth between the two objects as fast as you can for five or ten seconds. While doing the laser eye shift it is difficult to think of anything or be distracted by anything. As we know, when in the present we are not concerned about the past or the future. This technique is so simple and easy to execute, that an athlete can use it when needed. Prior to shooting the free throw, the basketball player can do the laser eye shift. The bowler and the golfer can do the same thing prior to the pressure shot.

Drs. Lee and Harrison developed the laser eye shift while working with the Kansas City Royals. They knew that the mind cannot process two sensory systems effectively at one time so they discovered a technique to emphasize visual dominance. This visual dominance, the eye shift, keeps the other sensory systems from interfering with the visual system. This lack of interference locks you into the present. When locked into the present, you do not have thoughts of the past or thoughts of future results.

VISUALIZATION TEST

This test comes from the book SEE IT & SINK IT. Dr. Farnsworth has the student look at the picture below. The student then closes his eyes and with a pen marks a line from the start to the finish. When the student feels he has reached the finish then the eyes are opened. The student is not allowed to trace the path with his fingers or pen while looking at the path. Good visualization traces an accurate path. Poor visualization leaves the path.

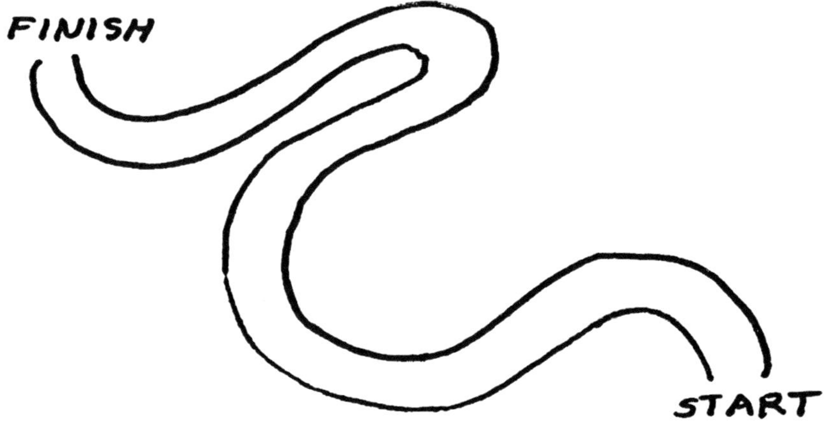

Dr. Farnsworth gives an interesting aspect to visualization for the test, as well as for all visualizations. He says when looking at the path, let the eyes move along the path, from the start to the finish, at the same speed as your hands would move the pen. Visualize to the same time frame as in real performance. When the basketball player visualizes his shot for the free throw he should visualize it in real time. The golfer should visualize the putt rolling in his mind at the same speed as on the green. Visualize to real time.

SELECTIVE ATTENTION

Farnsworth claims that a loss of concentration is the result of letting our sensory system attend to other senses, rather than to the visual sense. In other words, we are not being selective with what senses are focusing. The greater the pressure, the greater the chance of the other senses interfering with the visual sense. A golfer, visually focusing on the distance of his putt, may let a sound from the gallery interfere with the visual distance aspect of his putt. The audio sense is competing with the visual sense to cause distractions to the golfer. As stated earlier, one cannot process two sensory systems effectively at the same time.

When the pressure is on, we try so hard to do our best that we think too hard to make sure we do everything correctly. The last few moments in a match often create the pressure to cause the conflict of sensory systems. When the pressure is on, we must let our visual sense dominate and then act.

The feel process (a tactile sensory system) is now under investigation by many researchers. It seems that when an athlete focuses on feel they leave the visual sense. Focusing on the feel aspect often causes muscle tension, because the athlete is trying too hard to capture the feel aspect through the manipulation of muscles in order to feel. We use vision to determine distance and then try to make our muscles react to the distance. This is difficult to do as we have two senses competing with each other.

Feel is an interesting aspect of skill execution. In most cases, the feel of the skill is felt after the execution. A baseball/softball batter feels the impact when the ball is well into or out of the infield. The golfer feels the ball when the ball is over 15 yards down the fairway. By the time sensations run up the body to the brain, the ball is long gone. This is why in most striking skills the feel is after the impact. So one has to wonder how important feel is. This is radical thinking. Maybe feel relates to confidence?

Dave Pelz had golfers putt while wearing ski mitts. The ski mitts were to take away the feel aspect. He found that the golfers putted the same with the ski mitts on or with their bare hands. Have a student toss pennies, or a rolled up ball of paper, to a target. The first few tosses are concentrated on feel. The next few throws are concentrated on vision only, by seeing the target, and then tossing to the target. The vision-only technique will give better results, because the sense of vision tells the muscles how much force is needed. Vision makes the decision. If we let the conscious mind do the thinking as to how hard to toss the object, the muscles can get confused. Trust the visual aspect. Thinking about the importance of the situation or the skill, or thinking about winning or thinking of the results of the situation, will over-ride visions direction to the target.

"Thinking and analyzing while you are seeing doesn't really help; in fact, thinking hinders the seeing process. (W. Timothy Gallwey, THE INNER GAME OF GOLF).

Mihaly Csikszentmihaly, in his book FLOW (Harper Perennial,1990) gives us a quick insight into the importance of attention. "Attention is our most important tool in the task of improving the quality of experience. But, it is impossible to enjoy a tennis game, a book, or a conversation unless attention is fully concentrated on the activity." This is not an easy skill. In fact, Csikszentmihaly claims that contrary to what we believe, the normal state of the mind is chaos. Attention is only good for a short time frame. Discipline of the mind is required to lengthen our attention span. The greater the pressure or stress, the greater the potential for chaos in the mind.

OPTIMAL EXPERIENCE (FLOW)

Csikszentmihaly also talks about the optimal experience which is the flow state people achieve when they perform in what is often called a supernatural experience. He says that the optimal experience, and the psychological conditions that make it possible, seem to be the same the world over. Athletes when explaining this state of optimal experience, all seemed to give a similar description of how it felt. Long distance swimmers, chess players, mountain climbers, musicians and ghetto basketball players all shared the same feelings.

Csikszentmihaly found that the optimal experience has eight components. People in this state usually describe one or more of these components, but the majority experience all eight.

1. The experience occurs when there is a chance of completing the task.
2. Concentration must take place.
3. The task has clear goals
4. The task has immediate feedback.
5. The performance is effortless with no distractions.
6. A sense of control on their actions.
7. A concern for the self disappears but reappears after the experience.

8. Duration of time is altered. Everything seems to move in slow motion.

TWO THOUGHTS AT SAME TIME

Thinking two thoughts at the same time is counterproductive. As previously mentioned, the athlete must focus on one thing (the primary thought). In the dying moments of a match, many individuals make big mistakes by trying to focus on two or more things at the same time - the result of thoughts converging. The golfer may be thinking of winning, what the opposition is doing, how to play the shot, etc.

PATIENCE

Joe Hyams gives some interesting aspects to the importance of patience and being patient in crucial situations.

"You must learn to allow patience and stillness to take over from anxiety and frantic activity for the sake of doing something." So many times in the crucial last stages of a match individuals have lost their advantage through panic and frantic activity. The panic causes rushing, chaos and a brain dead process.

"The good player is patient. He is observant, controlling his patience, and organizing his composure.

When he sees an opportunity he explodes." Too many athletes explode before the opportunity, forcing to make things happen. Have patience. Boxers do not continually throw punches. They wait. Explore. Read their opponent. When the opportunity presents itself they strike. When you do not wait for the opportunity, you are playing into your opponent's moment of strength, moment of readiness and moment of strong defense.

"The same thing applies to problems in life. When a problem arises, don't fight with it or try to deny it. Accept and acknowledge it. Be patient in seeking a solution or opening, and then fully commit yourself to the resolution you think advisable."

Patience is particularly important in the dying holes of a match. No matter how few holes are left, the good ones have patience. They do not panic. REMEMBER: when you lack patience you become your enemy, a powerful enemy.

INSTINCT and CHOKING

Bobby Jones, the great golfer, was asked what he relied on when making an important golf shot. "Instincts. Instincts I honed after practice combined with playing. The more I depended on those instincts – the more I kept conscious control out of the mind – the more nearly the shot came off the way I visualized it. Concentrating on the results of a shot, to the absolute exclusion of all other thoughts, especially about its method, is the secret to every good shot I ever hit. The ability to play the shot you visualized and let trouble take care of itself is a rare quality in a golfer, one the average player should strive for more than perfection in a swing that may be beyond his capabilities anyway."

Bobby made one more statement that is especially interesting. He said, "I say from experience that 'choking' is caused by not using your own instincts." (BE THE TARGET by Byron Huff. Contemporary Books, Inc. 1996). When you start to think about how to execute, you eliminate your natural tendencies or instincts.

Instincts develop our feel for the skill. When we visualize the skill, our body is able to sense the required force and feel for execution. Basketball shooting, bowling, golf, etc all develop the feel through the visualization process. Jack Nicklaus claimed that visualizing the shot, sensing the target and swing needed to react to the picture is 50% of the shot. (BE THE TARGET by Byron Huff. Contemporary Books, Inc. 1996)

David Feherty, the world famous golfer and now a TV commentator, gives an interesting explanation of choking. He says, "Absolutely everyone has done it. It's not what happens to you that matters in the long run. It's your attitude. That's what determines how you cope with the next experience that comes along. . . Quite often it's how you deal with failure that determines how you achieve success. . . The mental process is like building a muscle. It's not letting your whole framework of thinking fall down around you. It's having the resolve and mental toughness to take it on the chin, keep your head up, and feel good about yourself for having done that. You can either feel bad because you failed or good because of your positive reactions to it. That will give you the armor to cope with it the next time." (David Feherty in MIND UNDER PAR).

BELIEFS

YOU WILL BE WHAT YOU BELIEVE

John Kehoe, in MIND POWER INTO THE 21ST CENTURY, talks about how you will become whatever you consistently think about yourself. You are responsible for your own self-image and you are responsible for creating and maintaining it. Settle for nothing less than a firm belief and conviction. Believe that you will succeed even if you have suffered past defeats. Forget the defeats. Forget the failures. They are just feedback for more learning to succeed. The following is from his book.

"Timid thoughts create a timid person.

Confident thoughts create a confident person.

Weak thoughts create a weak person.

Strong thoughts create a strong person.

Thoughts with a purpose create a person with purpose.

Visionary thoughts create a visionary person.

Thoughts of helplessness create a helpless person.

Thoughts of self-pity create a person filled with self-pity.

Enthusiastic thoughts create an enthusiastic person.

Loving thoughts create a loving person.

Successful thoughts create a successful person."

INTUITION

Many times we do things because our belief system tells us it is the right thing to do. We have no logical reason why we have this belief, we just know. It is often called intuition. Intuition is not a haphazard thought process. The thought process functions from the wide base knowledge of experiences. We may not recall the experiences, but for some reason we know the answer. Our knowledge and experiences give us the answer. The more knowledge and experiences we have, the better the intuition and the better the decision.

The athlete must get all the facts, and then let the facts sit on the mind by forgetting the facts and waiting for the subconscious to give the answer. The answer will come. This seems impossible and contradictory, but did you ever try to think of someone's name, couldn't remember it so you just forgot about it only to find it pops up to you in a short time, when you were not even thinking about it. This is how intuition works. The answer is there. We just have to let the subconscious mind give us the answer.

Sometimes intuition is called "a gut feeling" because we can sometimes feel the answer in our stomach. The feeling is a minor stomach irritation, a slow knawing, a feeling that is almost unexplainable, but there. We feel it. We act on it.

THINGS ALWAYS GO WELL?

Peter Dobereiner in Golf Digest (Nov. 1980 p.22) assesses the athlete's thoughts during practice times before their events. He is writing about golfers but the philosophy is the same for other sports. Peter claims that bad players cling to the belief that everything is going to go well and will practice accordingly. The really few good players know that bad things will happen and will prepare for it. They practice possible bad outcomes. He tells of golfer Peter Thompson, who would play his practice round like a novice hitting shots into the rough, traps, bunkers, etc. Actually, he was preparing himself for possible bad outcomes that may come up during the tournament. There must be some merit in this approach as Peter Thompson won golf's British Open five times.

COMPETITION

Many people are against sports because of the competitive nature of the games. Such people do not like the winning and losing aspect. They claim people should not suffer the pain of defeat. Life is competition. We are always competing with our life style for more health and enjoyment. Some of the most cutthroat business people are against competition in sports. This is ironic. Isn't the dating game and choosing a spouse a competitive thing? The problem is not in the competition but the way it is learned or taught. Competition is not about winning and losing, although this does happen. Competition is about bringing out your best. If you win you win. If you lose you lose. The point is, 'did you do your best against the competition'. Competition brings out the "Honor your opponent by doing your best".

Many people prefer the cooperation games, instead of the competitive games. Actually the competitive games are cooperation games. Both opponents honor each other by doing their best. This means each cooperates into helping the other to do their best. This makes the competition rewarding and valuable. Winning means little if the opposition gave up and quit. We have all experienced that winning is more fun, more enjoyable and more rewarding when the opposition was good and they gave their best. We are performing to overcome obstacles and distractions set up by the opposition. The challenge is to overcome the obstacles. Get your mindset to hoping your opponent can give you his best shot. Do not wish him ill. Let him do good so you can over-come his best.

What is actually happening is that competition is not against the opposition. Our opponent is not the enemy. Our opponent is there to make us do our best. Competition is with ourselves, not the opposition. Can we control ourselves to play to our maximum performance? The more the challenge by the opposition, the more we test ourselves. This means the opponent is not our enemy. Our friends, our parents, our teachers, our bosses, are our opponents. These people make us do our best. We honor them by doing our best.

Steve Prefontaine, the world class runner, explained it wonderfully when he asked his coach, Bill Bowerman, "If I run my worst and win or I run my best and lose, what does it mean?"

"The challenges of competition can be stimulating and enjoyable. But when beating the opponent takes precedence in the mind over performing as well as possible, enjoyment tends to disappear. Competition is enjoyable only when it means to perfect one's skills: when it becomes an end in itself, it ceases to be fun."(Mihaly Csikszentmihaly)

NEED TO WIN

The need to win is an overemphasis on results and is extremely detrimental to the skill. The need to win kills the moment, playing to the moment. It is nice to win and everyone should play to win. The need to win becomes an obsession and obsessions have a tendency to cloud the mind and hamper performance.

EXPLAINING THINGS

“If a wise person must explain something, he usually explains briefly. But behind that brief talk may be profoundly penetrating thought.” (BEYOND THE KNOWN by Thong Dang. Charles E. Tuttle Co. 1993). Coaches and teachers must learn to do this. Too many coaches/teachers are too verbal. They think that the more they talk, the more they are profound. Good coaches know how to explain things quickly and to the point. They talk in pictures so the players can easily understand.

Some coaches feel that to emphasize a point they have to raise their voices, yell and scream. This may work if it is only used occasionally, but if it is overused it loses it value. Be careful with this technique. Good coaches know when to use it. Weak coaches over use it and become ineffective.

CAN? Or CAN’T?

“If you believe you can or you believe you can’t, you’re probably right”. Henry Ford has received credit for this statement but others have made the same statement before him. Anyway, whoever said it made a profound and wise statement. The power of belief is still not reached it limits with athletes. Some have it. Most do not. In the book THINKING BODY, DANCING MIND their assessment is so good that we give it to you now.

“You need to work to renounce your restrictive beliefs about what you can and can’t do in sport. Your power as an athlete starts with the awareness that you have unlimited potential once you align yourself with the belief “I can”. Remember that acting “as if” you can achieve self-direction and not self-deception. It places you on the road of excellence. As you forge ahead, you can learn from your setbacks and mistakes.”

Hard opinions about yourself distort the truth about your potential. The Tao teaches you to be flexible in your beliefs: Rigidity will block your growth. THE TAO Te Ching (no.49) simply yet powerfully states: “Evolved individuals have not fixed mind.” Fixed mindsets obscure the unlimited boundaries of your potential. Keep your mind open; keep the Beginners Mind.

Most athletes on all levels of play, from the recreational enthusiast to the professional, utilize less than half of their potential to achieve. Why should you believe anything other than “I can”. Approach each free throw, putt, pitch, fly ball, pass, stroke, spike, or technical maneuver with a positive inner belief of yes – act "as if" and activate your concentration, confidence, and courage.

The Tao teaches us to neutralize an extreme force with the opposite force. Fight fire with water, fight anger with love, and fight "I can't "with" I can". Our ability to neutralize extremes gives us the power to alter reality. Beginning to believe you can, rather than you can't, is your ultimate power to alter your game and win. Simply act "as if" you can."

Acting "as if" is easy. Get your model and then act or behave like it. Actors do it all the time. They just make believe they are someone else and then act the part. A player can model another athlete they like. Actually, the player may take an animal, like a cat, and imitate their cat-like moves. It is easy but it takes practice.

R.L. Wing in his book THE ART OF STRATEGY (Doubleday, NY 1988) says, "Your inner opponents greatest advantage is your lack of belief in your ultimate triumph. "

William James, the famous American psychologist claimed that the biggest discovery of his time was that people's belief determined their life style.

Tim Gallwey in his book THE INNER GAME OF TENNIS said much the same thing as the other two people when he claimed that no factor affects performance more than the image the athletes have of themselves.

POSTURE

It is readily noticeable that one's posture reveals one's attitude. Poor posture may show laziness, lack of interest and other disharmonies. Good posture shows alertness, readiness, happiness, positiveness, and many other things. When acting 'as if' you are a winner, or successful, your posture will reveal this. Many positive people make sure their posture is very good when they are unhappy or depressed. The good posture is one way to fight bad thoughts and feelings.

ONE DAY AT A TIME, ONE GAME AT A TIME, ONE INSTANT AT A TIME, ONE SHOT AT A TIME.

This is the basic philosophy of Alcohol Anonymous. Their training is to live one day at a time. Forget the past and do not worry about the future. Just get by this day without a drink. Tomorrow, just do the same thing and the future will take care of itself.

This philosophy can apply to sports. Just play for the moment. Do not worry about the future. Do you best for the moment. Many distance runners and endurance event athletes do this. They do not focus on the outcome or why they are running such a long distance. They just perform to the moment - just one mile at a time. A good mile to the pace required. No fear of the future.

Focusing on the moment clears the mind for only one thought. There are no distractions about the future or past. Take care of each moment to the best of your ability and each moment will add up to your best total performance.

BUT

In THINKING BODY, DANCING MIND, George McClendon, a psychotherapist, gives an interesting philosophy of doing what you want in life. He claims that you should "stay to the left of the 'but' word." I would like to play golf today but I'm too tired. Go with the left of the statement by going to play golf. Naturally one must be careful of taking this to the extreme. I would like to play golf today but I will lose my job may be a strong enough reason to not play golf. Within reason the idea does seem to make sense and in many situations it would be good.

EXPECTATIONS

Expectations are preliminaries to pressure, anxiety, and disappointment. With an expectation we are under pressure to make it happen. We force our way to meet our expectations. Pressure and anxiety often go together. If we don't meet our expectations, then disappointment may set it. No expectations – no pressure. No forcing to meet demands. We do our best and then let it happen. Expectations force us to think and perform to the future. We become outcome conscious.

ANYTHING

"I do not hope for anything

I do not fear for anything

I am free."

This quote is the epitaph of Nikos Kazantzakis, author of ZORBA THE GREEK. (from THINKING BODY, DANCING MIND)

OPTIMISM and HOPE

Optimistic people see failure as only a need to change something to achieve success. Success is there, and it can be had. A pessimist sees failure as permanent. Good athletes have optimism. They need it. Sports and activities is a constant struggle with success and failure. The good ones rise with their level of optimism to overcome failure.

In 1984, Martin Seligman, did a study at the University of Pennsylvania using 500 freshmen. He found that optimism was a "better predictors of their freshman grades than their SAT scores and high-school grades." (EMOTIONAL INTELLIGENCE by Daniel Goleman, Bantam Books, NY 1995). Perhaps this means coaches should look at the optimism factor in their athletes.

C.R. Snyder, a University of Kansas psychologist, found that in his study the actual achievement of freshmen students were determined better by a test in the measure of hope rather than the SAT scores. (EMOTIONAL INTELLIGENCE by Daniel Goleman. Bantam Books, NY 1995).

Seligman also did a study with MetLife Insurance to demonstrate the power of optimism. Selling insurance is a battle with rejection and turn-downs. He found that the optimistic salesmen did better than the pessimistic salesmen. In their first year the pessimistic salesmen dropped out at twice the rate of the optimist. Seligman persuaded MetLife to accept the new recruits who scored high on the optimism test but failed MetLife's normal screening process. This group outsold the pessimists by 21 percent in their first year and by 57 percent in their second year.

The factors of hope and optimism seem to have a strong correlation with success. Hope and optimism keep the athlete going through the difficult times. Failure is not permanent, just a temporary setback. What is it that gives some people optimism and hope? Perhaps the biggest factor is motivation to succeed. Strong motivation is not a quitting motivation.

WISHING

Wishing is not the same as hope. People with hope strive to make their goals occur. People who wish just sit and wish it would happen.

SELF-EFFICACY

Optimism and hope are factors of the belief system. Albert Bandura, a Stanford psychologist, sums up the belief system. "Peoples beliefs about their abilities have a profound effect on those abilities. Ability is not a fixed property; there is a huge variability in how you perform. People who have a sense of self-efficacy bounce back from failures; they approach things in terms of how to handle them rather than worrying about what can go wrong.

(EMOTIONAL INTELLIGENCE by Daniel Goleman. Bantam Books, NY 1995).

SKILLED NON-ATHLETES

"We don't usually think of musicians or artists as athletes; yet nearly all of them show the same courage, mental focus, and highly-coordinated physical skills demonstrated by those who devote the same long hours to sports training. Dancers are among the hardest-working athletes, even though they seldom engage in formal competition." This quote is from the excellent book by Dan Millman. (THE INNER ATHLETE. Stillpoint Publishing, NH 1994).

People in the arts are like athletes. They practice long and hard. They practice more than many athletes. Musicians and ballet dancers are prime examples. Skill learning is skill learning, whether the skill is in sport, dance, or music. The movement of the bow on the violin and the throwing of a football are both highly coordinated physical skills, tempered with mental skills. The ballet dancer and the gymnast both go through similar physical skills. The arts are sport. Sports are the arts. They are one. Both are beautiful and captivating. Both are to be admired.

NUTRITION

A good diet is important and this book does not go into this aspect. A good diet is usually sufficient for athletes. Perhaps the most important factor of the diet is that a diet cannot replace good training. The principles of overload, specificity, strategy, and the laws of science must train the body. Diet cannot replace these principles.

LUCK

Don't count on it, but be prepared if it happens. Luck is like wishing for something good to happen. We wish for the other team or player to make a mistake, so we can gain an advantage. Sometimes it happens. If you wish for luck then you have not done the proper preparation. Prepare and execute. Do not plan on luck.

Many athletes have been told they were lucky. Their reply is "the harder I practice, the luckier I get."

SLEEP

The body needs rest. Sleep is the best way to rest. Too much sleep can be detrimental as it makes the body listless. Athletes on road trips sometimes get too much sleep during the day before competition. This can hamper performance. Not only does the body become slow but the mind also becomes slow and dull.

Lack of sleep the night before a contest, often presents little or no problem. If the body has been well rested throughout the week, this one sleepless night will present no problem. Many athletes do not sleep well the night before competition and they perform well by game time. They were well rested before competition.

SUPREME CONFIDENCE

"Supreme confidence comes from intelligence and knowledge not from bravado." (Bill Russell of the Boston Celtics in a TV documentary on HBOPE 9:00am Sunday, March 11, 2001). Maybe if more athletes believed and practiced this we may have less trash talk and bravado?

DREAMS

Are dreams believable? Do dreams give us a message? The study of dreams in recent years seems to give a yes to both these questions. Many athletes have seen problems solved in their dreams. Many athletes have seen their dreams realized. Jack Nicklaus has claimed to have solved several swing problems through his dreams at night during tournaments. He is not the only one. Writers and coaches often wake up in the middle of the night to record ideas on a notepad beside their bed. To have a notepad beside the bed tells us that the person is ready for these ideas at night during sleep. The note pad tells us they believe in dreams.

What are dreams? Dreams are visualization or imagery in the mind while asleep. Some say dreams are the subconscious talking to the mind. The mind talks in pictures so the dreams are pictures or visualizations. We know dreams work while sleeping so perhaps visualization during the day should work.

"Dreams precede reality; they nourish it, perhaps even create it." (IN PURSUIT OF EXCELLENCE byTerry Orlick. Leisure Press, Champaign, IL 1980)

ENERGY REVERSAL

Jim Brown of American football fame said, "When people try to hurt me, it makes me stronger. I take in that negative energy, run it through my system, and throw it back at them."

"Success is how far you bounce back." (on CNNSI television. March 25, 2001, 9:28 am EST).

CHARACTER

HONESTY

Some years ago the author was watching tennis on television. A player served the ball and the umpire called it out. An argument ensued by the server, but as usual there was no change in the call. The player served again but the receiver did not move to play the shot he just let it go by for the point to the server. The receiver knew the server's previous shot was good and the umpire was wrong.

This showed a lot of class. The real good ones have it. They do not need cheap points to win. They want to win on their ability.

KILLER INSTINCT

Killer instinct is well explained by Dr. Robert Rotella (GOLF DIGEST March 1985 p.70). He claims that most people think killer instinct means bearing down, trying extra hard, try anything, etc. Actually, killer instinct is staying composed, consistent, doing the right thing despite the pressure or situation. Confidence prevails.

ACCEPTING IT

Good athletes make mistakes but they are good because they accept the mistake and carry on. They do not sulk, cry, and/or whine. If need be, they will do extra practice to correct the mistake so it does not happen again. After the mistake – it is over with. You cannot change it, so do not dwell on it. Forget it. Accept it. Be alert. Get focused. Continue. Seve Ballesteros had the best solution for forgetting the bad shot – “instant amnesia”

POISE

Poise is controlled by emotions. No matter how devastating the situation, the good ones have the poise to handle the situation. Their confidence may be stressed, but they will not be consumed by distractions. They have prepared for the unexpected or bad situations. They will not succumb. The less skilled athletes are not skilled in emotional control even if they possess the mechanical skills. Emotions are a distraction to skill execution. If you can walk a 6-inch wide plank on the ground without falling off, then why can’t you walk the same plank 100 feet above the ground? Emotions. The fear of falling is the emotion. Emotions are one of the most powerful detriments to skill learning and execution. And yet, emotions can be one of the most powerful factors in learning. Learn to pick and choose your emotions. It can be done.

A REFLECTION OF YOURSELF

Tim Gallwey (THE INNER GAME OF TENNIS) makes an interesting statement in his book. “If you view an erratic backhand as a reflection of who you are, you will be upset.” This is so true in all sports. A bad backhand does not mean you are a bad person. A missed free throw, does not mean you are a klutz. A strikeout does not mean you are the worst of players. There is no meaning to the backhand other than you may have made a mistake or you haven’t learned the backhand yet. Great players have made backhand mistakes, so what more can you expect. Accept it. Do not dwell on it. Detach it from your mind and continue with the game. Later practice the problem.

THE EGO COACH

Too many coaches are suffering from ‘ego-itis’. Some are so concerned about their ego that winning comes in second. Amazing, but true. Many coaches are information databases. They just pass on information, more than enough. If enough information flows out of their mouth, then they think people will be impressed with their knowledge. This is not coaching. This is ‘ego-itis’.

Good coaches are insightful. They look beyond the basic information format. They look for the key move to correct several other mistakes. A ten year old can tell you to “do this”, “do that”, but this does not correct the problem. The good coach knows what will work or won’t work with this individual. The good coach sees down the road. The good coach sees what will work when pressure is present. The good coach sees the skill from the perspective of the student. Too many coaches coach to what worked for them, so naturally they feel that it will work for everyone. Good coaches use all their knowledge and experience to get inside the brain of the student. The coach feels the student’s body and thinks the mind of the student. The coach becomes the student.

EMOTIONS

Traumatic or terrifying emotions leave a stronger impression on the mind than common occurrences. In applying this to sports, it is recommended that the player make a successful skill execution very emotional. Show joy and excitement so that your success registers in the mind for future needs. Do not get emotional over your bad experiences; let them fade away - just forget’em - instant amnesia. If you get emotional over your bad experiences then they become too easily remembered. When you come to difficult playing decision, your mind will recall your past successful experiences instead of the bad experiences.

When you have a bad playing experience and you have an emotional reaction, chances are you will replay the experience over and over in your mind. Each replay reinforces the behavior and ingrains it stronger in the mind. If this works with bad experiences then why not use the same technique for good experiences. Get a good strong emotion of that successful experience, and let it replay on the mind. Let it reinforce the good behavior.

Emotions taken to the extreme can cause thinking and decision making problems, even if the mind has the facts for completing a task. The task is called 'working memory' and is stored in the prefrontal cortex of the brain. Strong emotions like anxiety, anger, arousal, winning obsession, etc., cause neural static (poor signals) from the limbic brain area (emotions) to the prefrontal cortex area. These poor signals sabotage the working memory in the prefrontal cortex and so the person can't think straight.

This is why we preach for the athlete to keep their emotions under control. Often, a player has the strategy or skill well learned, but come game time, or during phases of the game, the skill or strategy is forgotten or poorly executed. Emotions become so strong that the working memory of the skill or strategy cannot be executed properly because of the static or interference of signals coming from the limbic system. The decision-making process is flawed and functions poorly because of the interfering signals. The athletic terms 'be cool' or 'be calm' not only make sense, but they are valuable traits to have.

IMITATION

Many studies have shown that emotions often transfer to other people. It seems we unconsciously imitate the emotions we see displayed by someone else. This would seem to go with mob violence or softer mob actions, when people say that they did not know why they went with the crowd. This is why coaches and leaders must show calmness and be in charge of their emotions. This sets the example for the players or followers. It is a powerful factor. It is better to see a sermon than to hear a sermon. Set the example.

EMOTIONAL BREATHING

Dan Milllman gives an excellent account of how our breathing is affected by our emotions. He claims that to control and master our emotions, we must control our breathing. "The three primary emotional obstructions – anger, sorrow, and fear are each characterized by an imbalance in breathing. Anger is reflected by weak inhalation and forceful, exaggerated exhalation. Sorrow (as in sobbing) is characterized by spasmodic, fitful inhalation and weak exhalation. Fear can result in very little breathing at all." Recognize these breathing patterns and change the patterns into a controlled deep and even breathing pattern. Control your breathing patterns and you can control your emotions.

"Breath is closely connected to the well-being of the mind. Watch your breath. You will discover that when your breathing is short and shallow, your mind is restless. When you breathe deeply, your mind will become calm and tranquil and your intellect sharp and focused." (THICK FACE, BLACK HEART by Chin-Ning Chu).

Well, you have it all now. How do you feel.

Confident. Not a false confidence that I previously had. I now have the knowledge for a self-assured confidence. A quiet confidence. A damn good feeling. I am now confident in how I can attack the future for each shot. Golf Whisperer, you come along at the right time.

Ahhh... in Zen they say, "When the pupil is ready to learn – the teacher will come".

LaVergne, TN USA
28 December 2009

168213LV00004B/45/P

9 781608 441471